'I'm the Principal'

Principal learning, action, influence and identity

Stephen Dinham
Kerry Elliott
Louisa Rennie
Helen Stokes

amba press

Published in 2025 by Amba Press, Melbourne, Australia
www.ambapress.com.au

First published in 2018 by ACER Press, an imprint of
Australian Council for Educational Research Ltd

© Stephen Dinham, Kerry Elliott, Louisa Rennie, Helen Stokes 2025

This book is copyright. All rights reserved. Except under the conditions described in the *Copyright Act 1968* of Australia and subsequent amendments, and any exceptions permitted under the current statutory licence scheme administered by Copyright Agency (www.copyright.com. au), no part of this publication may be reproduced, stored in a retrieval system, transmitted, broadcast or communicated in any form or by any means, optical, digital, electronic, mechanical, photocopying, recording or otherwise, without the written permission of the publisher.

Cover design, text design and typesetting by ACER Creative Services
Cover image © Mainagashev, used under license from Shutterstock.com

ISBN: 9781923569287 (pbk)
ISBN: 9781923569294 (ebk)

A catalogue record for this book is available from the National Library of Australia.

Foreword

Each person who has been a principal of one or more of Australia's more than 9500 schools knows that there will be a time when the statement, 'I'm the principal' becomes wholly true. The title of this book recognises that, in different school contexts, each principal will lead with a unique combination of personal, professional and positional dispositions.

I'm the Principal eloquently explains that no matter how well prepared a person is to take on the role of the principal, doing the job and being the principal requires the individual to understand his or her own values and the values of those he or she works with. For those considering the role of the principal, this book, and the research that underpins its conclusions, provides deep insights into the ways of thinking, knowing and doing that are part of the privilege of being a successful principal.

The researchers have explored what it takes and what it means to be a principal, and, by doing so, they have extended their research beyond an understanding of principal practice to identify questions about the identity of individual principals as well as the principal collective more generally.

There is strong consistency in the responses of the principals in this book about their priorities and the importance they place on the core of their work – teaching and learning. This prioritisation is not only for themselves, but for the staff they work with, their students and, in the broadest sense, the community of their school.

The consistency in responses from the principals speaks to there being a collective principal voice in Australian schools that articulates the importance of instruction, evidence, student progress and achievement, school culture, and professional learning in informing critical principal priorities and perspectives. This voice is realistic and, at times, expresses a strong negative view of the increasing challenges of external compliance and management regimes that seem unable to cope with the rapidly changing context and complexity of schools.

The New South Wales Secondary Principals' Council has identified three sources of authority and accountability for principals:[1]
- professional authority – leading for learning
- community authority – leading for engagement and capacity building
- systemic authority – leading and managing the school.

This book recognises the tensions between these sources of authority, and provides a rich background and rationale for its research by reviewing the history and significant body of research into leadership in schools, especially those in Australia. The first five chapters of *I'm the Principal*, Part A, are dedicated to this.

The decision to construct the book and research using the framework of the Australian Professional Standard for Principals ensures that the project has a coherent research design and a clear, well-organised argument. The project findings are reported in Part B of the book; five chapters are based on the practices of the Standard and one chapter discusses the overall professional identity for principals: how principals form their own identity and make meaning of their work.

Chapter 6 discusses the importance of leading teaching and learning. In fact, leading teaching and learning, at the heart of the work of principals, and the subsequent focus of principal work in making a difference, articulating a clear moral purpose, and working with others to determine what needs to be done (and what does not), are themes that the research returns to throughout the book.

In Chapter 7, the principals recognised that, in leading themselves and others, they needed to know their strengths and the strengths of their teams. These principals have exemplified the confidence necessary to make mistakes, take risks and to be willing to disrupt practices that do not work. In doing so, they have described an investment of considerable time, resources and expertise in professional learning for their teams; a strategy that all the principals placed a very high priority. These principals understood that, more than almost any other profession in this country, teaching and

---

1   New South Wales Secondary Principals' Council, position paper, *The role, authority, leadership and accountability of the principal*, ratified at state assembly 26 November 2009, NSWSPC, n.p., 2009, p. 13.

school leadership have been subjected to political interference. Their responses belied their view that each school needs evidence from its own students, staff, school and community to not only indicate achievements and gaps, but also the progress made by students, staff and the school. They argued that schools need to tell their own stories, and there were very powerful responses from principals working in remote schools and schools for students with significant disadvantage; these principals understood the challenges clearly while continuing to love their work.

In Chapter 8, a chapter on leading improvement, innovation or change, the principals' responses focused on improvement, as many of the school and jurisdictional plans in Australia also do. This is perhaps one of the greatest challenges for principals and Australian schools, and there is a paradox between the deep discussions in other chapters about the impact of disruption, uncertainty and complexity, and the more cautious responses in this chapter.

Further, Chapter 8 illustrates an unspoken consensus from the principals that governments, educational institutions beyond the school, and system administrators need to take greater accountability for the decisions they make. This is because their decisions often limit school innovation to improvement and supplementary programs rather than the deeper reinvention and transformation found in other school systems across the world. If there are questions about whether Australian schools will continue to be successful in times that require greater innovation, there are much deeper questions about the ways governments fund and measure schools, about what educational innovations governments value for young people, and about the capacity of governments, systems and institutions to recognise the expertise of the profession in leading innovation, change and improvement.

Chapter 8 does give examples of principals and schools that have attempted significant innovation, but most of the principals interviewed acknowledged that strategies for improvement and innovation are often left to schools because jurisdictions have been less able to create and sustain broader innovation. Systems are often ponderous – they usually have planning framed ahead for 20–30 years while their layers of regulations, rules and compliance practices can be up to 20 years old. In this context, principals spoke like the boundary riders of an earlier history – determining who and what will be allowed through, and who and what will not. This is a tension all principals know as they work with their school staff and communities to respond to their current context – it is not the context of 20 years ago, nor is it a context 20 years in the future.

However, one inspiring metaphor was given by a principal working on Anangu lands, who described the historical divide and separation between the Anangu and white world views as being replaced by the Anangu view sitting within a larger circle of broader Australian education. The principal wanted to break through the circle to the global world beyond. In many ways this story represents what schools and school principals will need to do to understand and manage change and innovation. It is worthy of further research.

In Chapter 9, the research highlights how principals use data, systems thinking and strategy to lead and manage the school and community. All the principals identified the increasingly important operational role of school business managers or executive operating officers. With average annual budgets from $500 000 per annum (very small schools) to over $40 million, most of Australia's schools are small- to medium-size enterprises, where principals and their teams align operational practices to the educational nature of the enterprise.

Chapter 10 showed that principals still want their communities to be engaged and they appreciate the importance of student voice; there was an overall recognition that strategies were changing to achieve both of these priorities. Those interviewed shared useful suggestions for their colleagues, including a detailed discussion of the challenges of community engagement in technology-rich but time-poor communities.

In Chapter 11, a few of the principals spoke about the strategic partnerships they and their schools have with universities and not-for-profit organisations, but most emphasised the importance of principal associations, networks and mentors in their own learning. This highlights that the learning and professional nature of the principal's work goes beyond what is provided by employers and sectors.

Finally, in the last two chapters, Part C, of *I'm the Principal*, the authors discuss the overall findings of the 'I'm the Principal' project and celebrate the principal profession – something that many principals in this research would find awkward because, overall, they spoke of the professional collaboration and teamwork that is at the heart of school success.

The principals in this research recognise that the professional, community and leadership work of principals is poorly understood beyond schools, and that there is a need for it to be better represented in key forums and decision making. If this is to happen, the wider profession, the community and policy makers need to respect that when a principal says, 'I am the principal', their understanding comes with authority and professional expertise. The literature review and research for this book contributes to that knowledge, and will become an important reference for principal reflection and preparation.

Christine Cawsey AM
Principal
Rooty Hill High School, NSW

Acknowledgements

We would like to gratefully acknowledge the essential contribution of the 50 Australian principals from all states, territories, systems and sectors who generously gave of their time, experience and expertise to the 'I'm the Principal' project in 2016–17. Each one of you is a credit to your profession and we thank you for your commitment to your school, to education and to the broader community. It has been a pleasure and privilege to work with each of you.

Individually we would like to thank and pay tribute to the support we receive on an ongoing basis in our lives and work from family, friends and colleagues.

Table of contents

Acknowledgements   vi
About the authors   viii
Introduction   ix

■ PART A   THE PRINCIPALSHIP AND THE PROJECT

    Chapter 1   The role and importance of the school principal   2
    Chapter 2   Qualities, capabilities and actions of successful principals   14
    Chapter 3   Principal preparation, selection and development   23
    Chapter 4   Purpose and nature of the 'I'm the Principal' project   32
    Chapter 5   The principals: who are they?   46

■ PART B   'I'M THE PRINCIPAL': PROJECT FINDINGS

    Chapter 6   Leading teaching and learning   54
    Chapter 7   Developing self and others   83
    Chapter 8   Leading improvement, innovation and change   112
    Chapter 9   Leading the management of the school   142
    Chapter 10   Engaging and working with the community   158
    Chapter 11   Professional identity of the principal   172

■ PART C   OVERALL FINDINGS AND IMPLICATIONS OF THE 'I'M THE PRINCIPAL' PROJECT

    Chapter 12   Overarching findings of the project   184
    Chapter 13   Implications for the principalship: preparation, selection, workload, support and development   194

Notes   206
Appendix   213

About the authors

Stephen Dinham OAM PhD is Emeritus Professor in the Melbourne School of Education, the University of Melbourne. At the time of researching and writing this book he was Professor of Instructional Leadership and Associate Dean (Strategic Partnerships and Engagement) in the Melbourne Graduate School of Education at the University of Melbourne. He has over 40 years of experience as a teacher, university academic, researcher, writer and consultant. He has conducted a wide range of research projects in multiple areas of education including leadership and change, effective pedagogy, student learning and achievement, teaching standards, teachers' professional development and educational policy.

Kerry Elliott is a lecturer in Instructional Leadership in the Melbourne Graduate School of Education at the University of Melbourne. She is also a former Victorian public primary school principal and has 20 years of experience in schools. Kerry's research interests include educational leadership, school improvement and teacher professional learning. Her PhD research situates around factors that may facilitate effective use of the Australian Teacher Performance and Development Framework in schools. Kerry has worked within leadership programs for aspiring and established principals across Australia.

Louisa Rennie is Deputy Principal and Head of Senior School at Southern Cross Grammar, an independent, coeducational school in the western suburbs of Melbourne. She is currently undertaking research in educational leadership at the University of Melbourne. Louisa was the inaugural Director of Australian Principal Certification and, prior to that, the Manager at AITSL where she promoted the uptake of the Australian Professional Standard for Principals and led the design of the 360° Reflection Tool. Louisa has worked locally and internationally as a teacher, education adviser, deputy principal and acting principal.

Helen Stokes PhD is an Associate Professor in the Melbourne Graduate School of Education at the University of Melbourne. She is currently Associate Dean (Staffing) and the Academic Coordinator of the Master of Instructional Leadership program. Helen has over 20 years of research experience; her interests include developing professional identities, alternative education and trauma-informed education.

Introduction

We have all been teachers at various times, held various leadership positions in schools and other educational organisations, and engaged in providing leadership development and professional learning for teachers and school leaders across Australia and internationally.

We have researched and reported on various aspects of teaching, learning and leadership. We have all been involved in some capacity with the Master of Instructional Leadership program introduced at the University of Melbourne in 2013, and other educational leadership programs. We have presented courses through various leadership institutes serving educational jurisdictions across Australia, and we have presented on our research and work internationally.

Some of us have been involved in developing, evaluating and implementing various teaching and leadership frameworks and standards, including the Australian Professional Standards for Teachers and the Australian Professional Standard for Principals.

We have all taken a key interest in educational developments in Australia and overseas, including research and debate over education policies and practice, international and national student performance, the quality of teaching, and matters concerning equity and disadvantage.

A current international phenomenon is the increasing expectations being placed on schools to lift academic performance and to meet a wide range of social expectations; in this, school principals occupy a central and key role which is sometimes a lonely and exposed position.

Given this context, we determined as a team to investigate the work of the principal today through in-depth interviews with 50 principals from across Australia. This book is a record of that investigation and it contains many personal, first-hand comments, experiences, values, beliefs and concerns. It also speaks of the rewards and satisfaction of the role of the principal. These first-hand feelings and views are encapsulated in the book's title *I'm the Principal*, in that we are all, researcher and reader alike, introduced to these genuine and impressive professional people.

The subtitle of the book outlines the foci of this project: principal learning, action, influence and identity.

We hope you find the book interesting, informative and valuable, whatever your role may be.

Stephen Dinham
Kerry Elliott
Louisa Rennie
Helen Stokes

PART A

THE PRINCIPALSHIP AND THE PROJECT

CHAPTER 1
The role and importance of the school principal[1]

In today's climate of heightened expectations, principals are in the hot seat to improve teaching and learning. They need to be educational visionaries; instructional and curriculum leaders; assessment experts; disciplinarians; community builders; public relations experts; budget analysts; facility managers; special program administrators; and expert overseers of legal, contractual, and policy mandates and initiatives. They are expected to broker the often conflicting interests of parents, teachers, students, district officials, unions, and state and federal agencies, and they need to be sensitive to the widening range of student needs.[2]

Introduction

There has been a fascination with leaders and leadership throughout history. Even before written records, great leaders were the subjects of oral history and various means of depiction. However, while the study of leadership can be said to go back many thousands of years, the more formal studies of management and organisations only go back a little over a century.[3]

Today there is a plethora of publications, websites, courses, frameworks, institutes, regulatory bodies, consultants and standards devoted to leaders and leadership. Airport bookshelves are full of books purporting to reveal the six or seven secrets of being a successful leader, and an internet search of the term 'leadership' will generate more than three-quarters of a billion hits. Interest in the field of leadership is massive and global.[4]

Despite this fascination with leaders and leadership, the field remains something of an inexact science, as shown by the many leaders at various levels who fail to meet the expectations held for them. The corporate sector is infamous for rapidly appointing and turning over senior leaders, who often receive a golden handshake on appointment, large salaries, and a golden parachute when they are let go, all typically within five years or so. There are also frequent leadership failures in other fields such as politics and various forms of public instrumentalities.

The idea of a 'born leader' has been roundly discounted, as this chapter discusses, and since contemporary organisations emphasise the importance of leadership, there is an ongoing quest to discover what the attributes and actions of successful leaders are in order to inform leadership preparation, selection, appraisal and development. Indeed, the large amount of leadership books, reports, websites, training courses and models that are currently available to us is both indicative of the level of interest there is in these topics, but also of the uncertainty and dissatisfaction that exists within the field.

What is leadership?[5]

What defines leadership is important to consider prior to reflecting on its antecedents and manifestations in more specific fields such as education, and in more specific roles within this field such as the principal.

Various definitions over time have emphasised leadership:
- as a focus of group processes
- from a personality perspective
- as acts or behaviours
- as a transformational process
- from a skills perspective.[6]

Northouse has provided the following definition and components of leadership, which is useful when considering such approaches:

Leadership is a process whereby an individual influences a group of individuals to achieve a common goal.
Defining leadership as a *process* means that it is not a trait or characteristic that resides in the leader, but a transactional event that occurs between the leader and his or her followers. *Process* implies that a leader affects and is affected by followers. It emphasises that leadership is not a linear, one-way event, but rather an interactive event. When leadership is defined in this manner, it becomes available to everyone. It is not restricted to only the formally designated leader in a group.

> Leadership involves *influence*; it is concerned with how the leader affects followers. Influence is the *sine qua non* of leadership. Without influence, leadership does not exist.
>
> Leadership occurs in *groups*. Groups are the context in which leadership takes place. Leadership involves influencing a group of individuals who have a common purpose. This can be a small task group, a community group, or a large group encompassing the entire organisation ...
>
> Leadership includes attention to *goals*. This means that leadership has to do with directing a group of individuals towards accomplishing some task or end. Leaders direct their energies towards individuals who are trying to achieve something together. Therefore, leadership occurs and has its effects in context where individuals are moving towards a goal.[7]

Trait approaches to leadership

Our earliest conceptions of leadership came from stories and records of great historical figures, usually male, hence the nineteenth-century label 'great man theory' to explain and describe such leaders. Great figures from history and legend appeared to be larger than life in terms of personal and physical attributes, wisdom, bravery and accomplishments, so there has been an understandable tendency to regard these people as born leaders and incapable of being emulated by common people. Undoubtedly, some embellishment occurred through the ages of these leaders' characteristics and their deeds, and some may not have even existed, such as King Arthur and his knights of the round table. However, stories like the Arthurian legend have influenced our contemporary conceptions of leadership and the appropriate values, virtues and behaviour of leaders generally.

The 'trait' view of leaders, as it is sometimes referred to, was probably the first theory or approach to leadership. The personal characteristics that assisted these historical and legendary people to lead their followers and maintain their power often included height and physical strength, wisdom or intelligence, powers of oratory skill and persuasion, prowess with weapons (admittedly, acquired through long practice and expert instruction, but still usually vastly superior to others), resilience in the face of adversity, and in some cases the ability to foresee the future and exercise power over others through the dark arts of sorcery or by acting on behalf of a higher power.

Obviously, the trait form of leadership does not equate to Northouse's conception of leadership as a process and group function towards achieving a common goal. Additionally, the focus of the trait approach is more on the leader, than on leadership. The implication of this is that leadership is not open to all, and leadership capabilities are innate and cannot be learnt or developed.

Assigned versus emergent leadership and personal versus positional power

When we see a police officer on the street, a referee at a sporting event or a judge in court, it is natural for most of us to respond to the position held, rather than the person, who we may not know. We recognise the person's authority as being legitimate. Assigned leadership leads to what has been termed 'positional power'. However, in many settings, including schools, assigned leadership and positional power only takes you so far. When people ask for the reasons behind a decision, a response of, 'Because I'm the boss', 'It's my call', 'What I say goes', or even, 'It's my way or the highway', may not ensure the successful completion of a task and might prove to be counter-productive in the long run. This is where, in the case of effective leaders, earned, generated or 'emergent power' takes precedence.

Another distinction between assigned and emergent leadership is that in the latter, as people are respected and entrusted with greater responsibility by the leader, new leadership capability and 'personal power' can emerge from within the group of followers through what has been termed 'distributed leadership'.[8]

French and Raven have provided a typology of five bases of power that augments the previous discussion on personal and positional power:

1. *Referent power*: based on followers' identification and liking for the leader ...
2. *Expert power*: based on followers' perceptions of the leader's competence ...
3. *Legitimate power*: associated with having status or formal job authority ...
4. *Reward power*: derived from having the capacity to provide rewards to others ...
5. *Coercive power*: derived from having the capacity to penalise or punish others.[9]

Of the types of power bases noted above, referent power and expert power can be seen as aspects of personal power, while the remaining types can be seen to flow from positional power or assigned leadership. This is not to say, of course, that certain leaders might not draw their power to lead from several sources.

Leadership versus management

A perennial discussion in this field of study centres on the differences between management and leadership. English has commented upon the management/leadership binary in the context of education:

> The confusion between management and leadership continues to plague issues of preparation and performance in educational administration. Educational leaders do not perform in a social or organisational vacuum. Administrative positions exist within educational organisations, schools, colleges, and other related agencies. These positions are connected to other positions and to large organisational boundaries and functions. The dichotomy between leaders and management has become a point of contestation.[10]

Management does share commonalities with leadership. Managers also have leadership responsibilities in many cases, and leaders have management responsibilities. Each involves working with and influencing people in order to achieve certain objectives.

Kotterman has considered the differences between leadership and management. He begins by reflecting on the conventional, simplistic and dichotomist wisdom:

> Whereas leaders are seen as charismatic and often are admired and held in high esteem, managers frequently are thought of as the organisation's taskmasters with a whip in one hand and a bullhorn for screaming out orders in the other hand.[11]

But the reality is not so simple, as Kotterman makes clear:

> It is unusual for one person to have the skills to serve as both an inspiring leader and a professional manager. In large, complex organisations, these two distinct roles are even more difficult to assimilate in one person, and the tendency is to set leadership skills aside in favour of managing the workplace. Too often, senior managers believe they are leading when in fact they are managing ...
>
> This does not mean that managers cannot demonstrate leadership qualities. Managers may lead by example or lead a project or team, but they still end up

> performing the functions of management. Successful management is a really tough, challenging, and very important job. It should be given its due respect. Real leadership is tough, too, but it should not be confused with management.[12]

Kotter has also compared management and leadership, and notes that management is primarily about producing 'order and consistency', which is achieved through the key functions of planning and budgeting, organising and staffing, and controlling and problem solving. Leadership, on the other hand, is primarily about producing 'change and movement', which is achieved through establishing direction, aligning people, and motivating and inspiring others.[13]

We will now move to consider leadership in education, where the lines between management and leadership are perhaps even more blurred than previously suggested.

Leadership in education

There have been several distinctive waves of leadership conception, including educational leadership, over the past century.

As noted, earlier views and prescriptions of leadership were heavily influenced by portraits of great leaders – larger-than-life heroic figures that few of us could hope to emulate, but who we could all look up to for inspiration.

With the growth of formal (as opposed to traditional) organisations in the nineteenth and twentieth centuries, attention began to focus on matters of administration and governance, the finer details and functions of running an organisation. Weber's notion of 'rational bureaucracy'[14] in the early twentieth century was later influential, with the leader almost sanitised and homogenised through the objective application of standard tasks and organising procedures that governed the behaviour and work of everyone in the organisation from top to bottom.[15]

As our knowledge of organisations grew, models, theories and typologies of leadership were developed, and the notion of contingency, or fitting a type of leadership to a particular context or problem, was developed. In other words, the one-size-fits-all model of leadership was questioned.

In education, the study of educational administration was a wave that began in the 1950s and built sharply from the 1960s. In Australia and internationally, the late Professor Bill Walker was a major influence, with thousands of educational leaders completing courses in education administration, often by distance education, through the pioneering work in this field carried out at the University of New England in northern New South Wales; many other Australian educators made the trek to North American universities to study similar courses.

The next major development or wave in education occurred from the 1980s and resulted from the heavy influence of the corporate world of modern business. Business and management degrees exploded in popularity and degrees in educational management – as opposed to the earlier degrees in educational administration – began to appear. We saw much greater emphasis on educational strategic planning, quality assurance, mission and vision statements, value-added measures, measurable outcomes, management by objectives, competition, entrepreneurial activity and marketing schools. The language, techniques and mindsets of the corporate sector became pre-eminent in education at this time.

Meanwhile, there was a new wave building and it came out of the 'effective schools' literature of the 1970s. This new development went by the names of 'successful teaching', 'quality teaching' and 'pedagogy'. While educational management paradigms were dominant, work had been conducted in the background to look at what really added value in schools, and the answer wasn't management. Study after study and major meta-analyses confirmed that individual teachers made a major difference to student achievement, often working collaboratively in teams and supported by educational leaders. Suddenly, there was a realisation that the prime focus of schools was and should be teaching and learning – an absurd thing to have to say. Educational leaders had to refocus from managing their schools to being leaders of teaching and learning, to being 'instructional leaders'. New models and frameworks for quality teaching, productive pedagogy, and the like, came to prominence along with the use of professional teaching standards and, later, certification against these.

This is not to imply that educational management is no longer important, rather that we are seeing a new form of leadership. The management responsibilities for school leaders will not go away, but the most capable of school leaders are making their prime focus the leadership of teaching and learning, and they are empowering others through their leadership to revitalise and lift teaching and learning in schools.

Effective student welfare programs and procedures are seen to underpin academic achievement, with the two aspects not being dichotomous; there are high expectations for all. Educational leadership, both formal and distributive, is now seen as fundamental in creating the conditions where teachers can teach and students can learn. Leaders also play a key role in facilitating teachers' professional learning.

The principal as leader: the importance of the principal[16]

Attracting suitable applicants to the principalship

The importance of the principal to schools, teaching and learning will be outlined shortly, but it needs to be noted that, commensurate with greater recognition of the role and importance of the principal, it appears more difficult to attract suitable people to the role, quite possibly because of the increased expectations held for principals and the present-day challenges of the position.[17]

Leadership and student outcomes

Leadership is increasingly recognised internationally as a vital factor in improving school effectiveness, teacher quality and student achievement.[18] As a result, over the past 15 years or so, there has been greater attention paid to formulating professional standards,[19] models, profiles and frameworks for school leadership to articulate the breadth and depth of school leaders' roles, and to inform their professional learning, selection, appraisal and accountability processes.[20]

There has also been greater recognition that teachers exercise leadership.[21] As teachers become more experienced and adept in their roles, it is likely, indeed expected, that their leadership involvement and influence increases to move beyond the classroom to across the school, and, even more broadly, into the profession. This widening and deepening of leadership roles for teachers is recognised in the Australian Professional Standards for Teachers.

As noted earlier, principals will continue to be required to perform a variety of managerial functions, however, in considering their professional frameworks and standards, and its accompanying research, principals have been found to be most effective where they emphasise 'instructional leadership', that is, leadership for teaching and learning. Hattie concluded from his extensive international meta-analytic work that:

> School leaders who focus on students' achievement and instructional strategies are the most effective ... It is leaders who place more attention on teaching and focused achievement domains ... who have the higher effects.[22]

The crucial importance of the teacher to student learning has been long recognised.[23] The challenge for educational leaders is to make things happen within individual classrooms as well as across their school or area of responsibility. Wahlstrom and Seashore Louis have commented that:

> In the current era of accountability, a principal's responsibility for the quality of teachers' work is simply a fact of life. How to achieve influence over work settings (classrooms) in which they rarely participate is a key dilemma.[24]

Relative to teachers and teaching, principals have smaller measured effects on student learning for school-based factors beyond the classroom, yet the effects they have are still significant. Hattie has calculated an effect size of 0.39 for principals/school leaders,[25] and research evidence has confirmed that 'school leaders can play major roles in creating the conditions in which teachers can teach effectively and students can learn.'[26]

As a result of their extensive meta-analytic work, Marzano, Waters and McNulty have concluded that:

> A highly effective school leader can have a dramatic influence on the overall academic achievement of students ... Leadership has long been perceived to be important to the effective functioning of organisations in general and, more recently, of schools in particular ... a meta-analysis of 35 years of research indicates that school leadership has a substantial effect on student achievement, and provides guidance for experienced and aspiring principals alike.[27]

A key to understanding the apparent conundrum of whether educational leadership is important for learning or not, is to distinguish between different approaches to, or types of, leadership. Effective management of day-to-day school functions involving budgeting, facilities, teacher hiring and evaluation, planning and accountability can result in a well-run school, but if this is the extent or focus of leadership, there may be little effect on improving student achievement, at least at a whole-school level. This situation is what has led to calls for instructional leadership, or leadership for teaching and learning.

Robinson, Lloyd and Rowe have noted that:

> Instructional leadership theory has its empirical origins in studies undertaken during the late 1970s and 80s of schools in poor urban communities where students succeeded despite the odds ... these schools typically had strong instructional leadership, including a learning climate free of disruption, a system of clear teaching objectives, and high teacher expectations for students.[28]

Hallinger has proposed three dimensions for instructional leadership from his review of the field:
- defining the school's mission
- managing the instructional program
- promoting a positive school learning climate.[29]

He has also observed that attention shifted away from effective schools and instructional leadership during the mid-1990s and 'interest in these topics was displaced by concepts such as school restructuring and transformational leadership'.[30]

Transformational leadership goes back to James McGregor Burns' work on how some leaders 'engage with staff in ways that inspire them to new levels of energy, commitment and moral purpose'.[31] For a time, it became prominent and instructional leadership was relegated, and, to some degree, was discounted as outdated.

To compound matters, during the 1990s, there was great enthusiasm for system and school restructuring, and, as noted, for corporate models and approaches.[32] Yet, how schools are structured or restructured has been found to be a weak driver of improvement in student outcomes; despite keen interest in structural arrangements such as middle schools, mixed-ability groupings and 'open classrooms', it is the quality of teaching that occurs within these structures, and the leadership that guides and supports it, which is most important in improving student achievement.[33]

Too often schools make structural or organisational changes, in the hope that these will lead to improved teacher and student performance, without addressing the bigger issue of teacher quality and its impact on learning. A highly effective teacher can work within almost any structural arrangement, while a poor teacher will not suddenly become a good one due to some change in how their class or school is organised.

However, despite the enthusiasm for school restructuring and transformational leadership, the findings from international meta-analytic work, which compared the impact of various approaches to educational leadership alongside the wider developments and concerns over quality teaching and student performance, have caused a re-examination of the worth of instructional leadership.

In fact, Robinson, Lloyd and Rowe concluded from their meta-analysis of empirical work on the impact of various leadership approaches that:

> The comparison between instructional and transformational leadership showed that the impact [on student outcomes] of the former is three to four times that of the latter. The reason is that transformational leadership is more focused on the relationship between leaders and followers than on the educational work of school leadership, and the quality of these relationships is not predictive of the quality of student outcomes. Educational leadership involves not only building collegial teams, a loyal and cohesive staff, and sharing an inspirational vision. It also involves focusing such relationships on some very specific pedagogical work, and the leadership practices involved are better captured by measures of instructional leadership than of transformational leadership.[34]

Thus, while the need for instructional leadership had been formally recognised for three decades or more,[35] the approach has only regained prominence within the last 15 years or so. There is a growing focus on the importance of the quality of teaching to student achievement as revealed through international student testing regimes such as the OECD Program for International Student Assessment (PISA, introduced in 2000), Progress in International Reading Literacy Study (PIRLS), and Trends in International Mathematics and Science Study (TIMSS). As a result, instructional leadership is once more assuming centre stage. The 'league table' rankings and performance on such measures have increasingly become matters of concern and importance in many countries.[36] An international review by Barber and Mourshed found that:

> High-performing [i.e. the top 15 per cent of] principals focus more on instructional leadership and developing teachers. They see their biggest challenges as improving teaching and curriculum, and they believe that their ability to coach

others and support their development is the most important skill of a good school leader.[37]

Their review also established that a thorough knowledge of teaching and learning on behalf of leaders is essential if teachers are to be developed and supported in moving forward the learning of every student in their care: 'Leadership focused on teaching, learning, and people is critical to the current and future success of schools'.[38]

Additionally, Leithwood, Seashore Louis and Wahlstrom, in reviewing the research literature on leadership and school achievement, found that:

- The total (direct and indirect) effects of leadership on student learning account for about a quarter of total school effects.
- Leadership is second only to classroom instruction among all school-related factors that contribute to what students learn at school.
- Leadership effects are usually largest where and when they are needed most [that is, in the most challenging schools and circumstances, or coming off a 'low base'].[39]

Conclusion

Today, leadership is seen as central and essential to delivering the changes, improvement and performance society increasingly expects of all organisations, including schools. However, leadership, including educational leadership, is a more contentious, complex, situated and dynamic phenomenon than thought previously.

The relevance of distributed and teacher leadership in facilitating teaching and learning has been recognised, but the roles of the principal as a *leader of leaders* and a *leader of learners* has assumed even greater significance and importance.

In the next chapter, we will turn to the question of the attributes, capabilities and actions of those principals who are seen to be most effective in the facilitation of successful teaching and learning.

CHAPTER 2
Qualities, capabilities and actions of successful principals

There can be little doubt from an examination of research findings that leadership is important in developing effective, innovative schools and in facilitating quality teaching and learning, although as Sergiovanni has pointed out with respect to the Principal, 'their mere presence does not automatically result in the required leadership being provided'.[40]

Introduction

As noted in the previous chapter, leadership today is increasingly being seen as a group function, occurring when two or more people interact in the pursuit of some common goal or desired outcome.[41] Leaders of such groups attempt to find ways of influencing the behaviour of others, whether they occupy formal positions and/or are exercising their personal authority. This style of leadership is quite different from what might be termed 'command and control', which rests on line management, instructions and compliance.

Dinham has noted:

Recent research has shown that rather than being "strong" and decisive, effective leadership is intensely interpersonal, involving working with individuals and teams to "transform" teaching and learning. Leaders' relationships with their "followers" have thus assumed greater importance than the more technical aspects of administration, management and decision-making. It has been recognised that leaders need a sound understanding of human nature if they are to lead effectively. This is particularly the case in education where so much of what happens depends on collaboration, commitment, trust and common purpose. Thus, involvement of stakeholders, particularly teachers, is seen as a vital aspect of educational leadership. Notions such as "common vision", "mission", "empowerment", "beliefs", "values", "engagement", "commitment", "learning community" and "ownership" have increasingly been recognised as essential factors in educational leadership effectiveness, thereby leading to educational improvement and success.[42]

There is evidence that educational leadership generally, and principal leadership specifically, is vital in transforming teaching and learning, creating positive and innovative school cultures, improving teacher effectiveness, and enabling student learning and development. Therefore, the issue of preparing and selecting the right people to lead assumes great importance, as does providing them with ongoing support, constructive feedback and professional development, which will enable them to handle the complexities of the role while employing the strategies that have been found to have the greatest impact on teaching and learning.

Virtually every school has someone in the role of principal, yet we know that principal effectiveness can vary widely, as does teacher effectiveness. If we can better understand the attributes and actions of effective principals, it follows that we may be in a stronger position to assist all principals to improve their performance, and achieve the outcomes they and others expect of them.

This chapter is an attempt to synthesise current research findings regarding principal effectiveness and success, and the chapter that follows it considers the implications of this knowledge for principal preparation, selection and development.

What are the attributes and actions of successful principals?

One of the difficulties in understanding what constitutes a successful principal and how he or she operates is separating the idealised prescription – what people think an effective principal should be like and what he or she should do – from the research-based evidence on what a successful principal is really like and how he or she really works.

A secondary issue is the way success is defined and measured. Is it, for example, overall student achievement as measured by external testing? Is it a measure of value added or student growth on previous levels of achievement? Or is success based on a more holistic conception and measure, which encompasses academic, personal and social indicators, such as what is expressed in the Melbourne Declaration on Educational Goals for Young Australians?[43] After all, there are many high socio-economic status (SES) schools where external student test results are well above national and state averages, yet these schools are coasting and actually recording poor student growth. On the surface, they appear successful and therefore are implicitly thought to possess effective teaching and leadership.

Where lists of attributes of successful principals and their actions have been derived from research or anecdotally/intuitively, there is the danger of these being simplistically regarded as recipes or checklists for success. They also ignore the concentrated collaborative work and strategies that have been observed in individual contexts.

With the above caveat in mind, the following section is an illustrative selection of attributes and frameworks drawn from the findings of five projects.

Project 1: findings of the Wallace Foundation

The Wallace Foundation in the USA has conducted a range of studies and reviewed the research literature on school leadership, particularly principal leadership, in public schools over more than a decade. In a publication issued in 2013, it drew upon its work to identify five key practices of effective principals:

1. *Shaping a vision of academic success for all students*, one based on high standards.
2. *Creating a climate hospitable to education*, in order that safety, a cooperative spirit and other foundations of fruitful interaction prevail.
3. *Cultivating leadership in others* so that teachers and other adults assume their parts in realizing the school vision.
4. *Improving instruction* to enable teachers to teach at their best and students to learn at their utmost.
5. *Managing people, data and processes* to foster school improvement.[44]

Like other such lists, the above provides something of the 'what' of effective principalship, but is sketchy on the 'how' and 'why' behind these aspects, and in what way they are combined as part of an overall strategy.

Project 2: findings of An Exceptional Schooling Outcomes Project (AESOP)

As part of a larger project, Dinham identified the qualities and actions possessed and employed by principals at schools that had achieved outcomes well above those predicted by SES, and incorporated academic, personal and social indicators. The study encompassed 38 public secondary schools in New South Wales, Australia, that were found to be achieving exceptional or outstanding student outcomes in Years 7 to 10. The themes that Dinham categorised were:

1. *External awareness and engagement* – principals of schools where outstanding outcomes were identified exhibited a keen awareness and understanding of the wider environment and a positive attitude towards engaging with it ... Rather than perceiving a threat, principals are open to opportunities offered by change and engage with it. Even with mandated change, principals look for how they can adapt what they are already doing to meet new requirements.
2. *A bias towards innovation and action* – three broad approaches were discerned in the actions of the principals ... First, these principals use their powers and the rules and boundaries of the system creatively. Second, they exhibit a bias towards experimentation and risk taking. Third, they exhibit strength, consistency, yet flexibility in decision making and the application of policy and procedures.
3. *Personal qualities and relationships* – principals ... were found to possess and utilise high-level interpersonal skills and are liked and respected, often but not always by all. Their motives and actions are trusted by others ... Students, staff and community members speak positively of principals who are open, honest, fair, friendly and approachable. They value the fact that the principal will listen to them and hear what they say, thus showing respect.
4. *Vision, expectations and a culture of success* – these leaders possess a long-term agenda and vision, and are prepared to work towards this. They set meaningful, achievable goals rather than short-term targets ... These leaders identify and nurture the seeds for change and school improvement. They recognise and value the history of the school and use what has been achieved or what exists as a platform for further school improvement, thereby, releasing latent organisational energy.
5. *Teacher learning, responsibility and trust* – principals place a high value on teacher learning and fund staff development inside and outside the school. They model teacher learning, being prepared to learn from teachers, students and others. They release staff to engage in professional development

activities and bring others into the school to provide assistance. Principals said they 'never' turn down a legitimate and reasonable request for teacher development assistance.

6. *Student support, common purpose and collaboration* – in a high percentage of schools ... it was observed that principals often identify and utilise a central focus, e.g. ICT, assessment, literacy, pedagogy, student welfare. This priority area has resources diverted to it ... Programs to support and develop such areas bring members and parts of the school together, leading to better understanding and commitment and improved efficiencies and outcomes ... Student support is seen as broader than formal welfare and discipline policies and programs, and is every teacher's responsibility. Student support was found to have a predominantly academic focus of 'getting students back into learning', rather than being about 'warm fuzzies', or 'enhancing self-concept'.

7. *The core category: focus on students, learning and teaching* – the overarching theme emerging from analysis of data is the belief that the central purpose and focus of the school is teaching and learning. These principals and their staff recognise that every effort must be made to provide an environment where each student can experience success and academic, personal and social growth ... Principals of the schools where outstanding outcomes were being achieved were found to be relentless in their quest for enhanced student achievement. They do not become distracted and bogged down by the administrative demands of the principalship, finding ways to concentrate their energies on educational leadership. They constantly remind students, staff and the community that the core purpose of the school is teaching and learning.[45]

Project 3: findings from the National College of School Leadership

In a report for the National College of School Leadership, Matthews drew upon data derived from Ofsted[46] inspections, case studies and other empirical sources to profile highly effective headteachers (principals) who work with and through others, including teams of teachers in their schools.[47] Some of the attributes he summarised were:

- Clear pupil-centred vision and purpose ensured pupils reached their potential. Maximising young people's wellbeing and achievements was at the heart of these schools.

- Getting the best or most out of people was related to the philosophy, leadership approach and personal skills of the headteacher, including:
  - Motivating, encouraging, trusting and valuing colleagues to do well
  - Modelling, leading by example, especially in teaching
  - *Providing an opportunity* to undertake greater responsibility and undergo development programmes from the second year of teaching
  - *Promoting professional development* focused on teaching, learning and leadership, and keeping abreast of change; coaching is much in evidence
  - *Encouraging initiative* and allowing people – students and staff – to experiment, confident they will be supported
  - *Showing interest* and being generous with praise, encouragement and help in moving forward
  - *Knowing the names* of a very high proportion of learners; valuing and respecting them
  - *Being community-minded*, involving, consulting and being engaged within the local community
  - Building teams and empowering them.[48]

Matthews went on to conclude:

- The most effective leadership provides for CPD [Continuing Professional Development] of all staff, including structured opportunities for leadership development.
- As far as possible, effective leaders of learning apply the same principles, values and expectations to staff as to student learning, building a community of learners.
- The development of pedagogical leadership relies on effective modelling and shared approaches to planning, teaching, assessment, evaluation, support and intervention ... Pedagogical leadership development has a strong practice-based element. It has to be locally centred in schools of sufficient quality to host programmes.[49]

Project 4: findings of The Effective Leadership and Pupil Outcomes Project

The findings of The Effective Leadership and Pupil Outcomes Project conducted by Day and colleagues are consistent with the findings outlined above.[50]

In the words of the authors:

> The Effective Leadership and Pupil Outcomes Project is the largest and most extensive study of contemporary leadership to be conducted in England to date. Its sampling methods and innovative mixed methods design have enabled it to examine the work of head teachers [principals] and other school leaders in a range of primary and secondary schools nationally ... The study focused on schools that were identified to have significantly raised pupil attainment levels over a relatively short three-year period (2003–2005) ... Through a combination of statistical analysis of national data sets on pupils' attainment three groups of schools were identified, all of which had made sustained improvements in academic outcomes, but from different starting points. Low start, Moderate start and High start.[51]

The report authors made a number of claims based on the results of the project:

Claim 1 Almost all successful leaders draw on the same repertoire of basic leadership practices.
- building vision and setting direction
- understanding and developing people
- designing the organisation
- managing and supporting the teaching and learning program

Claim 2 The same basic leadership values and practices are enacted in contextually sensitive ways.
- leaders' experience [the less experienced head teachers instigated more change and accomplished more]
- school socioeconomic status
- school improvement group [emphasis, type, composition of group important].

Claim 3 School leaders improve teaching and learning indirectly and most powerfully through their influence on staff ability, motivation and the conditions of teachers' work.

Claim 4 School leadership has a greater influence on schools and students when it is widely distributed.

Claim 5 Some patterns of distribution are more effective than others.
- ['fatter', not 'flatter' distribution – the former achieved through consultation being most effective, the second and less effective achieved through delegation]

Claim 6 A small handful of personal traits explain a high proportion of the variation in leadership effectiveness.
- diagnosis and differentiation [diagnosis of needs, differentiating of responses and coordinating activities]

- values and virtue [the importance of leadership values of care, equity, achievement for all; high ideals and moral commitment].[52]

Project 5: findings from the Best Evidence Synthesis on School Leadership and Student Outcomes

Finally, in appraising the international research evidence, a major review of the impact of leadership on student outcomes utilising meta-analytic and other techniques was carried out for the New Zealand Ministry of Education by Robinson, Hohepa and Lloyd as part of the Iterative Best Evidence Synthesis programme.[53]

The report on the review was extensive, but one of the most illuminating findings was the distinction between transformational and pedagogical or instructional leadership.[54] Another significant and overall finding was the relative impact of five key leadership dimensions on student learning outcomes (see Figure 2.1).

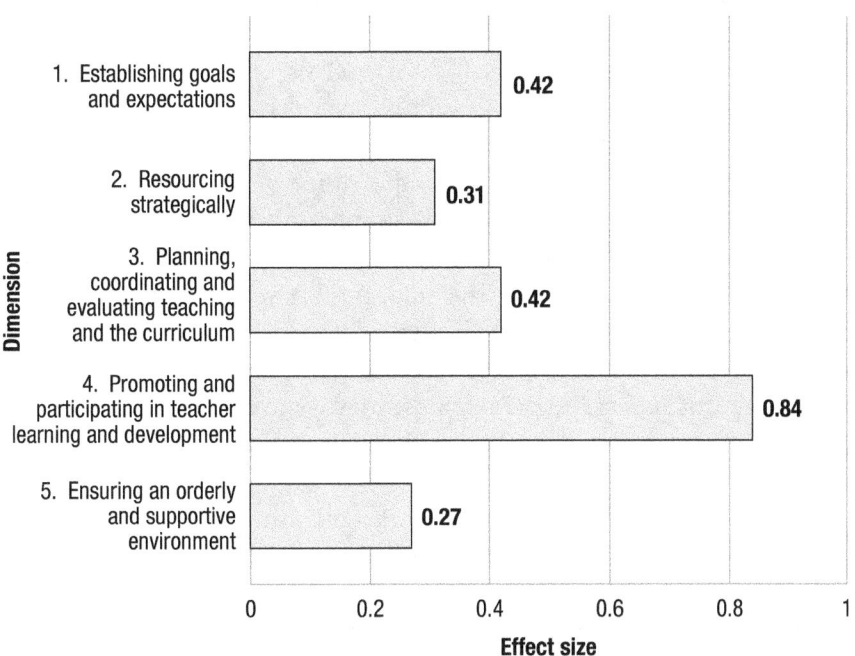

V Robinson, M Hohepa & C Lloyd, *School leadership and student outcomes: identifying what works and why*, New Zealand Ministry of Education, Wellington, New Zealand, 2009, p. 39

Figure 2.1: Relative impact of five leadership dimensions on student outcomes[56]

Drawing on their findings, Robinson et al., noted:

> Our primary conclusion is that pedagogically focused leadership has a substantial impact on student outcomes. *The more leaders focus their influence, their learning, and their relationships with teachers on the core business of teaching and learning, the greater their influence on student outcomes.*[55] [emphasis added]

Conclusion

The synthesis of findings outlined in this and the previous chapter point towards principals and other educational leaders being most effective in facilitating student outcomes when their prime focus is creating the conditions in which teachers can teach effectively and students can learn.

The most effective and successful principals maintain this central focus and uphold the belief that every student can learn. They have high expectations for themselves and for others. They are authoritative leaders, being highly responsive and demanding of those they work with.[57]

Effective principals realise the importance of classroom teaching, and the importance of promoting, supporting and participating in teacher learning and development to improve the quality of teaching in their school. They model the qualities they expect from others, including a commitment to their own professional development.

The management responsibilities of principals are significant and important, but successful principals find ways to deal with these while striving to be high-impact instructional leaders. They are effective and strategic planners.

The most effective principals work with, for and through those who are engaged to teach and support students. Their professional and personal relationships are of great importance; principals need to be able to motivate, communicate and work productively with a range of individuals, groups and bodies inside and outside the school.

In the next chapter we consider what the research literature has revealed about the key questions of how best to prepare, select and support principals.

CHAPTER 3
Principal preparation, selection and development

> *Principals play a vital role in setting the direction for successful schools, but existing knowledge on the best ways to prepare and develop highly qualified candidates is sparse. What are the essential elements of good leadership? What are the features of effective pre-service and in-service leadership development programs? What governance and financial policies are needed to sustain good programs?*[58]

Introduction

Some people still hold that leaders are largely born and not made. A way you can critique this view is to reflect on your leadership capabilities, and how and why they have changed over your life and career.

For those of you who are or have been teachers, how would you assess your leadership effectiveness at the time you began teaching? You might have had previous leadership experience that provided some grounding and a measure of confidence to lead, but how would you assess yourself as a leader at that time?

Moving to the here and now, how would you assess your leadership effectiveness today, both in your current role and more generally? Once again, you may have leadership experience outside your teaching career that adds to your leadership capabilities and confidence.

Overall, what growth have you had as a leader, and who and what has been responsible for this? Was it largely an ad hoc, self-directed process of learning on the job, or were there more formal processes involved in developing your leadership experience and capacity?

The key questions from this analysis are: can the process of becoming an effective leader be enhanced, guided and facilitated? Can those considered to be good leaders develop their leadership capability further? And if so, how?

Developing successful principals

A major review of formal principal leadership preparation programs in the US was conducted by Linda Darling-Hammond and colleagues from the Stanford Educational Leadership Institute (SELI) for The Wallace Foundation.[59]

This case-study based report distinguished between 'pre-service' and 'in-service professional development' programs for principals. Successful programs were found to exhibit the features outlined below.

Features of effective pre-service programs for aspiring principals

The SELI report found the following common elements in pre-service programs:

- A comprehensive and coherent curriculum aligned with state and professional standards, in particular ... standards, which emphasize instructional leadership.
- A philosophy and curriculum emphasizing instructional leadership and school improvement.
- Active, student-centered instruction that integrates theory and practice and stimulates reflection. Instructional strategies include problem-based learning; action research; field-based projects; journal writing; and portfolios that feature substantial use of feedback and assessment by peers, faculty, and the candidates themselves.
- Faculty who are knowledgeable in their subject areas, including both university professors and practitioners experienced in school administration.
- Social and professional support in the form of a cohort structure and formalized mentoring and advising by expert principals.
- Vigorous, targeted recruitment and selection to seek out expert teachers with leadership potential.
- Well-designed and supervised administrative internships that allow candidates to engage in leadership responsibilities for substantial periods of time under the tutelage of expert veterans. [60]

Features of effective in-service programs for practising principals

SELI found that effective in-service programs had the following features:

- A learning continuum that operated systematically from pre-service preparation through induction and continuing careers and included using mature and retired principals as mentors.
- Leadership learning that is organized around a model of leadership and grounded in practice, including analyses of classroom practice, supervision, and professional development using on-the-job observations connected to readings and discussions.
- Collegial learning networks, such as principals' networks, study groups, and mentoring or peer coaching, that offer communities of practice and support for problem-solving.[61]

The SELI study established that the best in-service programs had well-connected learning opportunities, which were informed by clear teaching and learning, and set in sound theory and practice; the programs had a clear model of instructional leadership and were not an incongruent range of ever-changing, one-off workshops.[62]

Overall findings of the SELI study

The SELI research found that:

> Graduates of the exemplary programs who became principals were significantly more likely than the comparison principals to hold positive beliefs about the principalship and feel more strongly committed to it.[63]

The study demonstrated overwhelmingly the benefits of aspiring and practising principals engaging in: formal professional development, cohort-based programs built on the principles and knowledge of effective teaching, instructional leadership, and school change and improvement.

An Australian approach to principal preparation

The Australian Institute for Teaching and School Leadership (AITSL) has developed a range of resources, tools and frameworks to support school leadership development and school leaders' professional practice.

AITSL has made five major recommendations for preparing school leaders that are congruent with the findings of the SELI project outlined earlier.

1. **Take a systematic, standards-based and coherent approach.** To be effective, principal preparation must be systematic and coherent, based on clearly articulated professional standards. It should include the following elements:
   - a thorough appreciation of leadership demographics and trends – clear and shared understandings of the principal role, underpinned by professional standards
   - a focus on the attractiveness of the principal role so that teachers are eager to make the move into leadership
   - responsibility for identifying and preparing future leaders shared between employers, system leaders and the profession
   - structured professional development opportunities for aspiring principals that focus on leadership abilities.
2. **Identify and nurture talent.** In the best approaches to principal preparation, potential leaders are identified early in their careers and given a range of opportunities to develop their leadership skills. Successful succession planning requires:
   - structured, transparent career pathways
   - clear selection prerequisites for promotion.
3. **Match learning to an individual's capabilities, career stage and context.** Pathways to advancement should be clear, with professional learning appropriate to each level explicit, well understood and sustained after appointment ... To be effective, learning for aspiring leaders should occur in three broad stages:
   - developing deep and comprehensive pedagogical knowledge as the foundation for strong instructional leadership. This learning can be done relatively early in the journey to principalship as it is compatible with a teaching role
   - developing the many higher-order and interpersonal skills required by principals, including strategic thinking, change leadership, and emotional and social intelligence. This learning is best developed over time and should occur well before an aspirant takes on the role of principal
   - developing management skills. This learning is best undertaken immediately prior to assuming a principal role, as it can then be consolidated through immediate practice.
4. **Use evidence-based adult learning techniques.** Highly effective preparation programs reflect an understanding of a range of adult learning techniques that have been shown to be effective and provide a diversity of experiences over time. They include:

- discriminating application and selection processes matched to the learning opportunity
- spaced delivery, blended learning and the opportunity to apply new skills and knowledge, collaborate, gain feedback and receive ongoing support
- a degree of personalisation that takes into account the needs, career stage and context of the individual
- an emphasis on learning from experts and practitioners
- recognition for the learning undertaken.

5. **Evaluate programs for impact.** It is critical to engage in rigorous evaluation for purposes of accountability and improvement. Principal preparation programs should:
   - provide evidence of participant readiness to take on the role.
   - measure impact upon take-up of role.
   - demonstrate growth in the number of well-prepared aspirants available to take up future vacancies.[64]

The role of Professional Standards and Frameworks for Principals

Exemplary principal professional development programs utilise and are often built on professional standards frameworks. Dinham, Anderson, Caldwell and Weldon have noted the development and use of professional leadership standards:

> The first educational leadership standards – which were intended to capture the essence of educational leaders' work for a variety of purposes such as selection, professional development and appraisal – were developed in the 1990s in the US, the UK and Australia. These generally comprised exhaustive lists of competencies – atomised 'shopping lists' – encapsulating the duties of principals and other leaders. Such standards were positive in that they 'have helped inform the development and improvement of many leadership programs and policies.'[65]

However, Dinham et al. add that more recently:

> developed leadership standards have moved away from such competency lists to 'capabilities', the former now generally seen as unrepresentative of leadership roles, inflexible with regard to different occupational positions and career stages, and unable to adequately address ethical, moral and contextual issues in leadership.[66]

They note that:

> [c]ompetencies have also been criticised for being more about measuring performance 'now' than being aspirational in guiding and encouraging further growth.
>
> With the move from competencies to leadership capabilities, there has been a commensurate shift from use of the term 'standard' to the use of broader 'frameworks', some seeing standards as implying standardisation and with frameworks being conceived as more flexible and applicable to varied contexts and settings.[67]

Anderson et al. have commented that despite the flurry of activity in leadership standards and preparation programs in Australia, there are no formal requirements to become a principal yet; in most jurisdictions 'a four-year teaching qualification and [teacher] registration remain the only formal requirements for school leaders.'[68]

Preparation and selection of principals

There are two broad schools of thought when it comes to selecting candidates for the role of principal.

The first requires the completion of a mandatory formal preparation program before an individual is deemed suitable to apply for a principal position. This formal training in itself can either be open to anyone who meets some form of minimum requirements, i.e. basically self-selection or self-nomination, or alternatively, some formal programs for principal preparation also have selection methods to identify the most suitable candidates and/or those most likely to succeed in the program.

The second broad form of principal selection does not require the completion of a formal program of preparation or qualification. The latter is the situation commonly experienced in Australia, although the completion of a relevant optional preparation program might be seen in a favourable light when principals are considered for appointment.

The Wallace Foundation found weaknesses with self-selection for principal preparation programs, particularly where participants did not have to demonstrate suitability against criteria for both the program concerned and the principalship.[69]

The Hay Group surveyed existing formal, though not mandatory, principal preparation programs, and noted 13 examples from across Australian public and non-government school systems, indicative of the interest and perceived importance of the area.[70]

Of the programs examined by the Hay Group report authors, the following program dimensions were commonly present:
- Educational Leadership
- Interpersonal Leadership
- Organisational Leadership
- Emotional Intelligence
- Visionary Leadership.[71]

The capabilities that were in some programs, but not universal, were also noted in the report:
- reflective practice
- coaches and mentors staff
- has a personal commitment to life-long learning
- manages knowledge
- leads community values.[72]

A key consideration with offering principal preparation programs, whether mandatory or otherwise, is to determine the target group or groups. The Hay Group report has commented:

> One of the critical factors in the success of professional development programs is the identification of the appropriate target group. Scanning a number of programs for aspiring leaders suggests that they are generally targeting candidates early in their teaching careers. In Australia, this tends to be after five years of teaching experience. In the US, the required years of experience range from two to five years. Drummond (2008)[73] reported that there was a belief in the UK that aspiring principals needed to be identified and trained within their first nine years to ensure that succession needs are met.
>
> Aside from stage in their career, our research in Australia specifically found that the basis of the identification of the appropriate target group varies greatly depending on the state, sector and/or jurisdiction.[74]

At times, there might be specific target groups within the overall target envelope, including women, Aboriginal peoples and Torres Strait Islanders, and various minority or under-represented groups. These targets may be general or specific to certain schools.

There is an enormous number of published criteria and processes for principal selection from jurisdictions around the world.[75] Some include administrative steps, requirements and protocols, while others indicate the sorts of capabilities and values necessary for a particular state, system and/or school. Some criteria are standards based. In the US, for example, the Interstate School Leaders Licensure Consortium (ISLLC) has standards that have been adopted by the National Policy Board for Educational Administration and the Council of Chief State School Officers to form part of the selection process for principals.[76] A typical case study is the Kentucky Department of Education, which has formulated its guidebook for selecting a principal by incorporating the ISLLC standards.[77]

Australia has only had a national standard for principals since 2011, although there were many leadership standards in existence and use prior to that.[78] The use of the Australian Professional Standard for Principals is not binding in the preparation, selection or appraisal of principals, although its use is increasing and it does inform the processes of preparation, selection and appraisal of principals, alongside reflection, self-directed learning and more formal professional development. Some have proposed that the use of the Standard for principal certification become mandatory, but there are logistical, financial and constitutional barriers to this if an agreement across the states and territories cannot be reached.[79]

The peak cross-sectoral body representing principals in Australia is the Principals Australia Institute. In 2015, PAI conducted a national prototype trial utilising the Standard as part of a trial certification program, which involved existing principals and was directed by Louisa Rennie. The lessons from this trial will be important in any attempt to introduce either voluntary or mandatory certification of aspiring and/or practising principals.[80]

Conclusion

Principals today are vital to delivering the outcomes expected of schools. The influence of principals on the quality of teaching, and the learning and development of students has been found to be significant. Leaving aside out-of-school influences, the principal is second only to the influence of the classroom teacher on student learning.

The evidence is strongly in favour of the need for and benefits of identifying suitable candidates for the principalship, engaging such people in formal professional development programs, selecting principals based upon professional standards and associated capabilities, and providing practising principals with ongoing professional support and development. This is particularly important as attracting suitable people to the principalship is becoming increasingly difficult. A more systemic, developmental and supportive climate is needed.

In the following chapter we explore the background and nature of the 'I'm the Principal' project.

CHAPTER 4
Purpose and nature of the 'I'm the Principal' project

The role of the principal of a school in the twenty-first century is one of the most exciting and significant undertaken by any person in our society. Principals help to create the future. Principals are responsible and accountable for the development of children and young people so that they can become 'successful learners, confident creative individuals and active informed citizens'.[81]

Principals are the leading educational professionals in the school. They inspire students, staff and members of the community to continuously enhance the learning of all, and they continually strive to understand and improve their impact.[82]

Introduction
School leadership is increasingly being recognised as a vital factor in improving school effectiveness, teacher quality and student achievement.[83] As a result, more attention has been paid to formulating professional standards and frameworks for school leaders. This is so the breadth and depth of educational leaders' roles can be articulated, as well as to better inform the processes for professional learning, selection, appraisal and accountability.[84]

In considering professional standards for principals, while principals will continue to perform a variety of managerial roles, they are seen to be most effective where they place major emphasis on 'instructional leadership', that is, leadership for teaching and learning.

As previously noted in Chapter 1, Hattie states:

School leaders who focus on students' achievement and instructional strategies are the most effective ... It is leaders who place more attention on teaching and focused achievement domains ... who have the higher effects.[85]

Depending on their intended purpose, professional standards for leaders and school principals can play crucial roles. They can aid reflection and self-development, formulate suitable professional learning experiences, attract and select suitable candidates for positions of responsibility, and assess the effectiveness of school leaders. Standards also articulate the values, knowledge and practices of school leaders to the wider community.

The Australian Professional Standard for Principals

Australia now has a professional standard for principals for the first time.[86] This is the result of developmental work, which reaches back over several decades, and is a remarkable achievement in itself, given the context and history of Australian education. A key component of the Australian Professional Standard for Principals' success will be the degree to which it is seen as authentic, has utility and adds value to the education system as noted by Dinham who led the piloting of the APSP.[87]

The 'I'm the Principal' project used the Standard as a construct to consider the main contributors to principal learning, action, influence and identity through interviews with 50 practising principals drawn from various sectors and levels of Australian school education.

Background to the Standard[88]

An account of the development of the Standard has been provided by Dinham, Collarbone, Evans and Mackay, each of whom was involved with the process:

One of the challenges in formulating professional standards for principals is to capture the sheer diversity of the contexts in which they can operate: from teaching principals in small schools to those heading multi-campus schools; from low to high SES and low to high NESB; from urban to regional to isolated; from struggling, coasting to successful schools, and in government, other systemic and independent schools.

Years of largely discrete work by educational systems, professional associations and other bodies within Australia had resulted in many and varied leadership standards and frameworks being in use across the nation although a uniform national standard was lacking. In 2008, work on national leadership standards began. This was part of broader work around national professional standards for teachers which had an even longer history.[89]

Dinham et al. go on to say:

When the Australian Council for Educational Research (ACER) was contracted to conduct a mapping and consolidation of Australian leadership/principal standards for the Commonwealth Department of Education, Employment and Workplace relations (DEEWR), it examined more than sixty extant leadership/principal standards and frameworks then being used for a variety of purposes across the nation. This set was by no means exhaustive. Like others, ACER concluded that given developments in Australia such as national student standardised testing and a national curriculum, the time was right for a national standard for principals to compliment the national standards for teachers (at four career stages) and national accreditation of teacher education courses, developments advocated previously in a report for the Business Council of Australia.

When thoughts turned to developing national standards for leaders/principals there were conflicting views about their intended nature, audience and purpose: some advocated a generic standard for leadership, whilst others favoured a standard for principals or multiple sets of standards for aspiring, practising and even exemplary principals. A key point of disagreement was whether a standard for principals should be used for performance appraisal purposes (i.e. a performance standard) or as a guide for professional development, self-reflection and to inform processes such as promotion and appraisal (i.e. a content standard).

These debates were at times intensely political and some stakeholders were quite passionate about the superiority of 'their' standard(s). It should be noted that while much of education in Australia is funded directly and indirectly through the federal tax system, constitutionally, education is a state and territory responsibility, and thus gaining agreement for national initiatives in education is not easy. 'Whose responsibility?' and 'who pays?' are frequent refrains.

Over time, jurisdictions, employers, systems, professional associations and individual schools had also developed their own processes to guide, select, appoint and appraise school leaders. Some of these were underpinned or informed by

> leadership and/or principal standards and frameworks, but the terrain was quite muddy overall.
>
> Gaining universal stakeholder agreement for a National [now Australian] Professional Standard for Principals was not an easy task and represented a significant achievement. To compound matters, the timeframe to write the Standard and have it endorsed was extremely challenging.[90]

Once agreement was reached across the various jurisdictions, the Australian Institute for Teaching and School Leadership (AITSL) commenced work on the principal standard in early 2010, and drafting began in September that year. Dame Professor Patricia Collarbone from the UK played a key role in this work as an external expert and circuit breaker. AITSL also established an external expert steering group and an internal expert group, drawn from across stakeholders, to guide and support the work; there was an intensive and extensive process of research, drafting, critical review and feedback involving organisations and jurisdictions from across Australia.

The drafting of the Standard was guided by a set of principles:
- privilege the skills and knowledge specific to educational leadership
- reflect the complexity and changing nature of contemporary school leadership
- recognise the collaborative nature of school leadership
- encourage a futures-focused leadership capacity
- guide principal preparation, development programs and self-refection to meet the needs of school leaders in different contexts.

The initial research focused on current thinking about school leadership and standards for principals and leaders used in other countries, including the UK, Canada, New Zealand and the USA, as well as the range of standards already in existence in Australia identified by ACER.

From the outset, the research into school leadership highlighted the importance of school context, leadership practices, models of leadership and personal qualities, knowledge and skills. What also became apparent was the range of environments Australian principals operate within and the complexity, critical significance and interrelated nature of the role of principal. The first exposure draft of the Standard was developed to reflect these findings:[91]
- The school context in which the Principal works is unique and of critical importance. The size of the school, the age of

students, its traditions, location and other community factors mean that the Standard must be applicable to the diverse nature of Australia's schools. 'At the same time though, most of the evidence we have reviewed suggests that good leadership is the same irrespective of context, and that "what works" is surprisingly consistent.'[92]

- It should be focused on the primary task of the organisation, in this case, learning, teaching and student outcomes.
- The practices and competencies of leaders evolve as they move through their career, and their learning and development needs to reflect this as well as being available when and where they need it.
- Leadership is collaborative and distributed among members of school teams; it does not reside in one individual. The role of the leader is to orchestrate and engage with, and grow and develop, other leaders at all levels of the school.
- New models of leadership within and beyond the school are emerging with school leaders taking on a range of roles within their community.
- In order to improve the life chances of all students within the community and the nation, principals have a wider responsibility that involves developing the education system as a whole at local and national levels.
- Controversially, research shows that a small handful of personal qualities and skills explain a high proportion of the variation in leadership effectiveness.[93] Successful leaders draw upon the same repertoire of personal qualities and capabilities. This in turn explains a significant amount of the variation in leadership effectiveness.

In addition to this work there was extensive consultation with principals, parents' associations, academics, state officials, professional associations and other stakeholders from across Australia. This was not a one-off exercise but an iterative process that took place throughout the development of the Standard. The responses supported the key findings from the research; they reinforced the importance of context, the enormous diversity in schools across Australia and the systems in which principals operate, as well as the challenges that exist for the Aboriginal peoples and Torres Strait Islander populations, and others.

There was consensus that the purpose of the Standard needed to be clearly articulated and the language made accessible. Its contents required a focus on professional development, creativity and risk taking, and it should include self-reflection, ethics and values. The importance of relationships and working with others was also stressed by respondents.

Following the research and the first round of consultation, the conceptual model of the Standard was refined, and tested for completeness and clarity (see Figure 4.1 for the final model). It was critical that the model reflected the systemic nature of the role of principal, and was clear and unambiguous. Only then could the model be built upon and turned into an accessible and useable standard.

At this stage, the international panel of experts reviewed a draft of the Standard. Their feedback centred on the need to make the purpose of the Standard even more explicit: what is it for and what difference will it make? The panel also focused on what would be needed to increase the Standard's uptake and impact. There were further helpful suggestions related to leadership requirements, professional practices and language from the external international panel.

To road test the Standard, tenders were called for and nine organisations were selected by AITSL to undertake ten pilot studies under the direction of Stephen Dinham. While each project had a particular focus and context, each was required to specifically address three key research questions within a common research approach:

1. *Authenticity* – is the Standard authentic? To what extent does the Standard accurately define the leadership requirements and professional practice of effective principals? Does the Standard describe effective school leadership? Does the Standard provide a framework of the knowledge and skills of effective principals, regardless of context?
2. *Usefulness* – is the Standard useable? How well does it provide an effective framework for professional learning? How useful would the Standard be for planning professional development and reflecting on practice? How effectively could it help to inform strategies to attract, prepare and develop effective principals for leading 21st century schools? How useful is it as a guide to inform the management of self and others?
3. *Value-adding* – does the Standard value-add to the knowledge and skills of effective principals? Is the Standard fair and reasonable? Is it inspirational and aspirational? What evidence supports the Standard?[94]

A small but significant change took place as the conceptual model was developed and tested with stakeholders: the name changed from 'National Standards for Principals' to 'The National Professional Standard for Principals'; later still, 'Australian' was substituted for 'National'. The use of 'standard', singular, was in response to the consensus that the power of the model lies in the way it reflects the integrated and interrelated nature of the role of the principal – everything that principals do in their professional practice is underpinned by their vision and values, their knowledge, and their personal qualities, requirements common to all leaders. Research has shown that there:

> are statistically empirical and qualitatively robust associations between heads' educational values, qualities and their strategic actions and improvements in school conditions leading to improvements in student outcomes.[95]

Thus, the name change reflected the systemic or holistic nature of the role, which is not simply a list of attributes, duties or activities.

A principal's leadership requirements and professional practices are far more than a role description, duties statement or a lower-level list of person specifications. The leadership requirements and professional practices go right to the heart of the principalship, and what it means for a principal to be responsible for the life chances of young people in their school, community and society.

AITSL has described some of the essential features of the Standard:

> The Standard gives expression to the leadership, educational, and management requirements and practices of principals. The Standard is an integrated model that recognises all good leaders share common qualities and capabilities, which are expressed as three Leadership Requirements. Principals draw upon these three Leadership Requirements within five areas of Professional Practice.
>
> The Standard acknowledges the challenging and changing context in which principals work, and the diverse settings and variety of situations which they face on a day-to-day basis. The Standard provides a model against which principals can match their knowledge, qualities, experiences and skills to determine their strengths and areas for development. It is 'Standard' rather than 'Standards', as it is integrated by nature, reflecting the complexity of the role and its shared visions.[97]

The Standard is illustrated in Figure 4.1; a brief further explanation of the Standard follows.

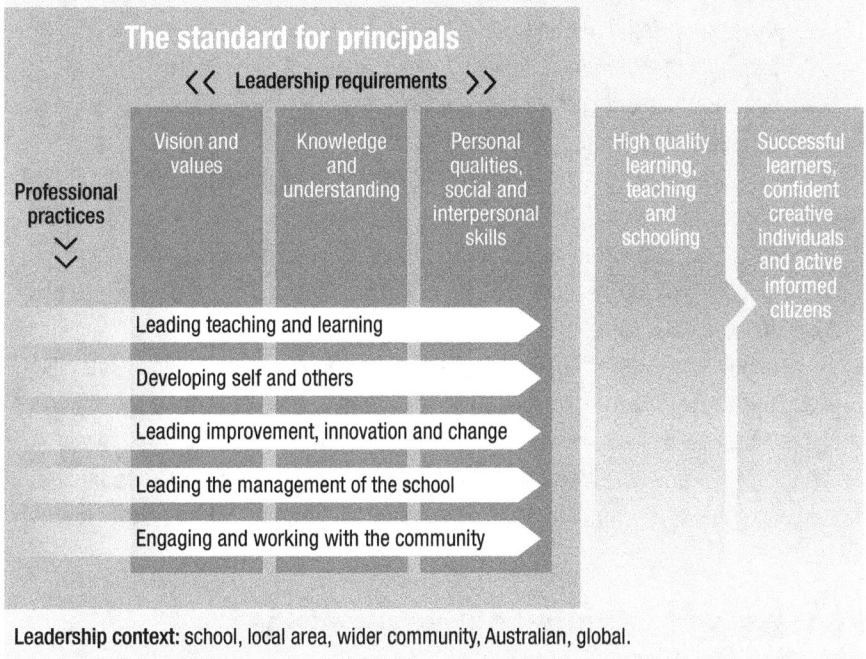

Leadership context: school, local area, wider community, Australian, global.

Australian Institute for Teaching and School Leadership, *Australian professional standard for principals and the leadership profiles*, AITSL, Melbourne, 2014, p. 11.

Figure 4.1: The Australian Professional Standard for Principals[96]

As discussed earlier, one of the key questions asked of the Standard's pilot during its road test was whether it would work within and across the great diversity of school settings found in Australia. In other words, whether it had authenticity, utility and added value. That the Standard 'worked' was confirmed in the pilot studies.[98]

Given the above key finding, AITSL has noted:

> The Standard is applicable to principals irrespective of context or experience. What will vary is the emphasis given to particular elements of the Standard as principals respond to context, capability and career stage.
> The Standard is based on three Leadership Requirements:
> 1. Vision and values
> 2. Knowledge and understanding
> 3. Personal qualities, social and interpersonal skills.

These requirements are enacted through the following five key Professional Practices:
1. Leading teaching and learning
2. Developing self and others
3. Leading improvement, innovation and change
4. Leading the management of the school
5. Engaging and working with the community.

The Standard details the Leadership Requirements and Professional Practices of principals separately. It is important to emphasise they are always fully interdependent, integrated and with no hierarchy implied. These requirements and practices will be reflected in the individual leadership contexts in which different principals work.

Although contexts differ, in all professions there are particular leadership expectations for those in senior roles. For those preparing to take up the role of principal, as well as current principals, it is important to consider ways of engaging with and developing an understanding of those expectations through the Leadership Requirements and Professional Practices of the Standard.[99]

Purpose and intended outcomes of the 'I'm the Principal' project

The overarching purpose in undertaking the 'I'm the Principal' project was to better understand what it takes and what it means to be a school principal today. As the preceding chapters discuss, much has been written about educational leadership, and various standards and frameworks have endeavoured to capture what effective principals are expected to know, understand and do.

While the Australian Professional Standard for Principals framed the study and the principals' interview questions, the focus of this project was on the people and their experiences within this construct. In other words, to look at principals in action across Australia's varying sectors, contexts and settings.

I'm the Principal is intended to serve a range of audiences and address their needs; the book gives considerable advice and lessons from experience, provides evidence of what it is like to perform the role, and is a useful guide for practising principals, aspiring principals and other educators. Further, in exploring the role of principals, their development and actions, *I'm the Principal* provides insights and evidence to researchers, and to those providing professional learning and support for principals. The book aims to be realistic rather than idealistic, so it offers guidance for system officials and policy makers, and may be of value to those more generally interested in the role of the principal.

As a reader using this book, you may be a principal or aspire to the position. Or perhaps you know a school principal – the one at your child's school, a colleague, a relative, a friend, or even one from a school you attended as a child. You may be in a position to see a principal engage in conversations, lead meetings and manage the day-to-day operations of the school, all to ensure a quality educational experience for every child under his or her care. It's also possible that you know little of the role, particularly what it encapsulates today.

The key purpose of *I'm the Principal*, therefore, is to provide an appreciation of what it takes and what it means to be a school principal. This is to better understand the influences on and processes of professional and personal growth and development, and to enable individuals to not just perform the role, but to flourish and gain satisfaction from it.

The researchers interviewed school principals from across Australia to investigate how each leader's identity as an educator and principal has developed, and what the influences, learning and experiences were that contributed to their current capabilities and needs. The project offered an insider's view of the role and so attempted to capture how each principal came to be where they are, what their work currently entails, what advice they would retrospectively offer themselves or to others in different stages of development, and, more generally, the relevance of their experience to systems and policy makers.

The 'I'm the Principal' project sought to establish aspects to principalship that are more universal than particular, and to describe what variables and possible contextual elements there are in the development for and performance of the role. This book does not, however, seek to prescribe a best way of leading a school, and it does not make sweeping generalisations or offer a simple recipe or checklist for success. Instead, the project record offers various perspectives of the principal role, and the attributes and practices current leaders draw on throughout their work in schools. As will be seen, there are commonly held values and principles that underpin and drive the work of these people, as well as common challenges and needs.

The work of a school principal is rewarding, but can be lonely; it is made up of brief encounters and regular interruptions, and is steeped in responsibilities and accountabilities yet may be free from accolades. Previous work in this field has highlighted that principals often feel that nothing really prepares them for assuming full and ongoing responsibility for a school, despite the various forms of preparation available or periods acting in the role.[100]

The 'I'm the Principal' project highlights the important and changing work of principals in supporting the development of others and enabling quality educational experiences for all students. In offering interesting and personal perspective, on educational leadership, this project aims to inform the development of future principals, provide opportunities for reflection for those in the role, and contribute to discussion among policy makers and system leaders about the skills and needs of our school leaders now and into the future.

Design and method

The 'I'm the Principal' project drew on qualitative methodologies since the aim of the study was to understand experiences, explore narratives and look for participant-defined meanings in regard to the role of the principal.[101] The project was conducted over an 18-month period and included a series of phases including project development, data collection, data analysis and write up. The project team met regularly to discuss and plan the project direction and later its progress.

The project offered accounts of principals' views and experiences, and aimed to:
- better understand what it means to be an effective principal
- inform the practice of being a principal
- examine how identity as a principal is formed
- enhance understandings of what it means to lead effective teaching and learning
- raise the status and regard for the role of principals through such better-informed knowledge, understanding and appreciation.

Two key questions were developed to guide the work. These were:
1. What are the key aspects and contributors to principal learning, action, influence and identity?
2. What informs the practice of being a principal and what does it mean to lead learning and teaching in a school?

CHAPTER 4: Purpose and nature of the 'I'm the Principal' project

Phase 1: project development
This included the development of the:
- project aims and guiding research questions
- literature review (of leadership, with a focus on educational leadership, and the Australian Professional Standard for Principals)
- sampling frame (to guide the selection of principals to be interviewed). Interviewees from the sample came from a range of different school contexts (early childhood–primary, primary, secondary and P–12 schools of different sizes, and special purpose schools), systems (government, Catholic and independent) and locations (rural, regional and metropolitan); a mix of female and male principals of different ages and experiences were selected (see Chapter 5)
- interview schedule (structured using the 'Professional Practices' from the Standard; refer to Appendix 1)
- ethics and research applications and approvals
- data collection, storage and analysis methods.

Phase 2: data collection
Structured interviews were selected as the method to gather the stories and reflections of the 50 principals. All interviews were conducted by phone and in two parts because of the length of the interview schedule; each interview took 45 to 60 minutes. The two interviews with each principal were conducted within a week. Principals were given a choice of timing; most elected to have a day or so between each of the interviews.

Heath, Brooks, Cleaver and Ireland have noted that all interview-based accounts are representations of particular situations or phenomena.[102] Interviews can, therefore, provide an insight into an issue from a specific context or perspective. In our work, we hoped to understand how principals can effectively enhance and lead learning and teaching in their schools. We drew on a wide range of principals from different school contexts, locations and systems, and selected principals who were able to bring different perspectives, experiences and contexts to their work as a principal. As McLeod comments, simply presenting the voice of the participants by describing what they have said is not enough, it is also important to bring together different perspectives and compare the experiences of the individuals across broader social patterns.[103]

We also hoped to understand how identity as a principal is formed. We acknowledge that this understanding is partial, contextual and shaped by how the principal may have been feeling at the time, but despite these limitations, interviewing does provide a glimpse of lived experiences when researching identity, as McLeod has described.[104] Chase notes that conducting interviews allows the stories that people tell to constitute the empirical material needed 'to understand how people create meaning out of the events in their lives.'[105] She further comments that this requires a conceptual shift on the part of the researcher, who has to move away from just seeing interviewees as providing answers for research questions, to interviewees as having stories to tell and a voice of their own. This was very relevant to our research as the interviewed principals have commented that the process has helped them to reflect on what they do; they appreciated having the time to talk about their background and, by being listened to and recorded through the interview process, they have been acknowledged for their work.

Phase 3: data analysis and write up

The generation of data through multiple individual interviews formed a process of triangulation of the data. Denzin has argued that triangulation reflects an attempt to gain an in-depth understanding of the phenomenon in question as many different points of view of the work of the principal from multiple contexts are brought together.[106]

In Phase 3, we used the Miles and Huberman[107] framework to analyse the data from the 50 school principals. This framework follows a four-step process:
1. data reduction
2. data display
3. identifying themes
4. verifying conclusions.

In the data reduction stage, we coded the interviews of each participant using the five 'Professional Practices' from the Standard as key themes or categories. These are:
1. Leading teaching and learning
2. Developing self and others
3. Leading improvement, innovation and change

4. Leading the management of the school
5. Engaging and working with the community.

Yin has proposed that linking the data to themes assists in keeping the analysis within the scope of the research questions.[108]

With the synthesised data, we moved onto the data display stage where we considered all the initial key themes and looked for patterns and interrelationships in the data. To assist us, we drew on the Standard's three 'Leadership Requirements' of:
1. Vision and values
2. Knowledge and understanding
3. Personal qualities, social and interpersonal skills.

The patterns and interrelationships identified in data display allowed for higher-order themes to emerge from the data that went beyond those first discovered during data reduction. These included the broader themes of principal professional identity and principal planning, action, influence and impact.

Finally, using step four of Miles and Huberman's framework, we drew conclusions by stepping back to consider what the analysed data meant with respect to the key questions, and we assessed the 'confirmability' of our data against leadership theory.[109] Therefore, we argue that this process of qualitative analysis is confirmable because it is credible, defensible, warranted, and able to withstand alternative explanations.

CHAPTER 5
The principals: who are they?

Introduction
The previous chapters have provided the background to the 'I'm the Principal' project. This chapter is an overview of the principals, their gender, their current type of school, location and sector, and their professional experience. As described in Chapter 4, for this project's research, 50 principals from diverse educational communities were interviewed for their insights and experiences. The Australian Professional Standard for Principals provided an organising construct for the interview schedule that was used, and a general framework for the analysis and interpretation of data that followed.

The principals were not intended to be truly representative of their system, sector or nation, but they did broadly represent a national cross-sectoral base of Catholic, government and independent schools. The principals were male and female, and worked in a variety of settings including small to large primary, secondary, special purpose and combined schools; they also provided first-hand experiences from their contextual settings in metropolitan, provincial, remote and very remote locations.

As researchers, we were grateful for the learning opportunity to hear first-hand from colleagues who bring wisdom, insight and experience to the complex work of leading educational communities.

Backdrop for the research
By way of background and comparison with the demographics of the principals in the study, the Australian Bureau of Statistics provides an overview of Australian schools, which is summarised below.[110]

In 2010, there were 9468 schools in Australia, comprising 6743 government schools (71%), 1708 Catholic schools (18%), and 1017 independent schools (11%). During that year, there were 6357 primary schools, 1409 secondary schools, 1286 combined primary/secondary schools, and 416 special schools. Excluding special schools, 70% of schools were primary, 16% were secondary and 14% were combined primary/secondary schools.

In 2010, there were 3 510 875 students in Australian schools spread across NSW (32%), Victoria (24%), Queensland (21%), Western Australia (10%), South Australia (7%) and Tasmania, the Australian Capital Territory and the Northern Territory (combined 5%). During that year, there were 62 831 students who identified as Aboriginal peoples and Torres Strait Islanders.

Approximately 66% of Australian school students attend government schools, 20% attend Catholic schools and 14% attend the remaining independent schools.

In 2010, there were 286 135 full-time equivalent teaching staff employed in Australian schools, comprising 183 725 teachers in government schools and 102 410 teachers in non-government schools. Females constituted the bulk of both primary (81%) and secondary (58%) school teachers.

Overview of the principals

What follows is an overview of the principals, their professional experience, their current type of school, and its location and context.

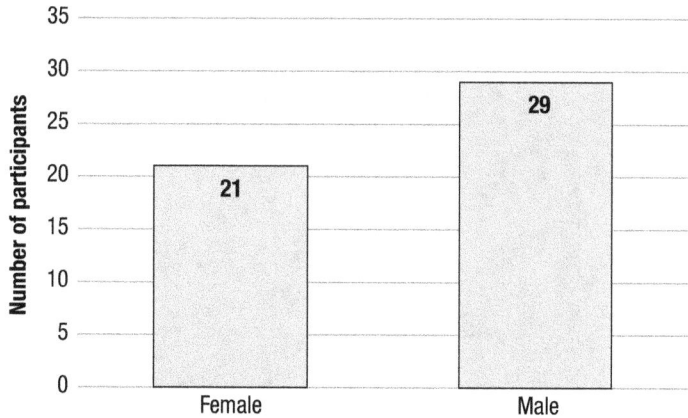

Figure 5.1: Principal participants by gender

Figure 5.1 indicates that a total of 21 female and 29 male principals were interviewed. Figure 5.2 shows that the 50 principals came from all three sectors in the Australian educational context: government,

Catholic and independent schools. The principals were not asked at any time to represent the voice or opinion of their respective system or sector, but rather to share their insight and experience as an educational leader. Some of those interviewed had worked across sectors.

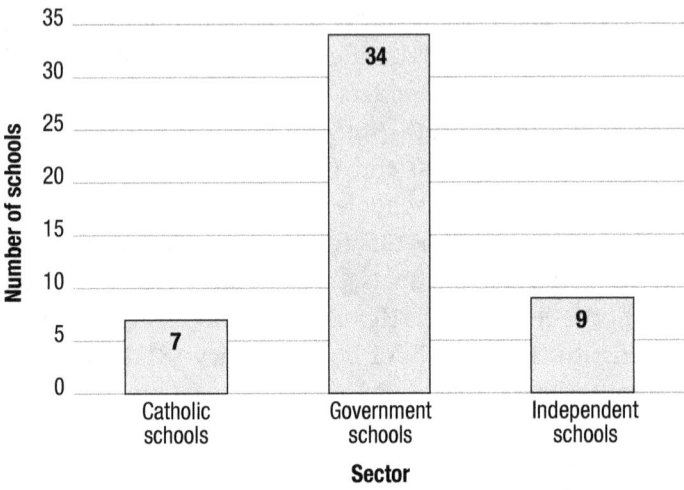

Figure 5.2: Schools by sector

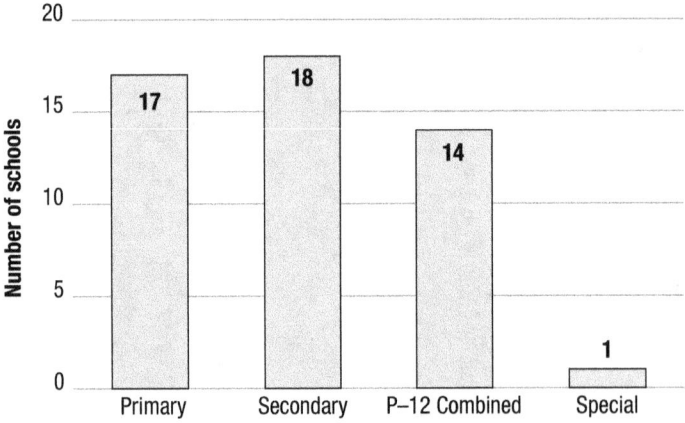

Figure 5.3: School type

Figure 5.3 defines the school type as derived from the My School website (https://www.myschool.edu.au/) and sets out the type of school where the 50 principals worked at the time of the interviews. School education in Australia comprises 13 years. Primary schooling usually comprises seven years, beginning (variously termed) in kindergarten (K) / preparatory (P) / reception (R) and ending in Year 6. Secondary schooling starts in Year 7 in all states except in South Australia, where it currently starts in Year 8. Secondary schooling ends in Year 12 although compulsory attendance ends earlier.

There were 17 principals from primary schools and 18 from secondary schools. There were 14 principals from combined schools, comprising a mixture of primary and secondary year levels. One principal was from a special school, catering explicitly for students with special and/or unique educational needs. A school designated as special or special purpose by its school authority caters for students with mental or physical disabilities or impairments, slow learning ability, social or emotional problems, or students in custody, on remand or in hospital.

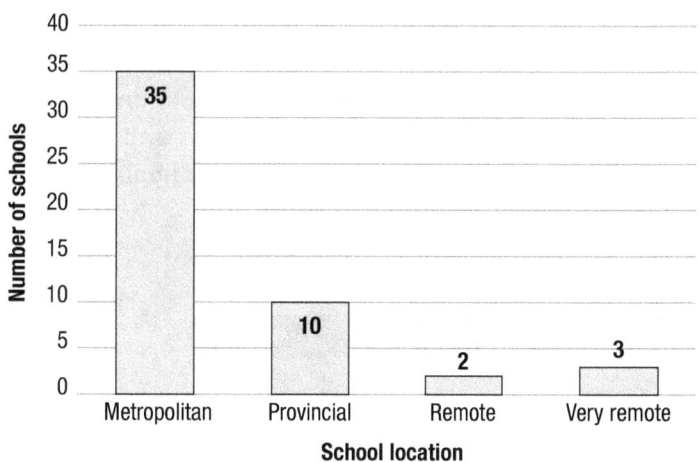

Figure 5.4: School location

Figure 5.4 gives the school locations of the principals; designations are also derived from the My School website. My School uses four main classifications to define the location of schools: metropolitan, provincial, remote and very remote. The location is determined according to the Schools Geographic Location Classification Scheme of the former Ministerial Council for Education, Early Childhood Development and Youth Affairs (MCEECDYA), now the Education Council.

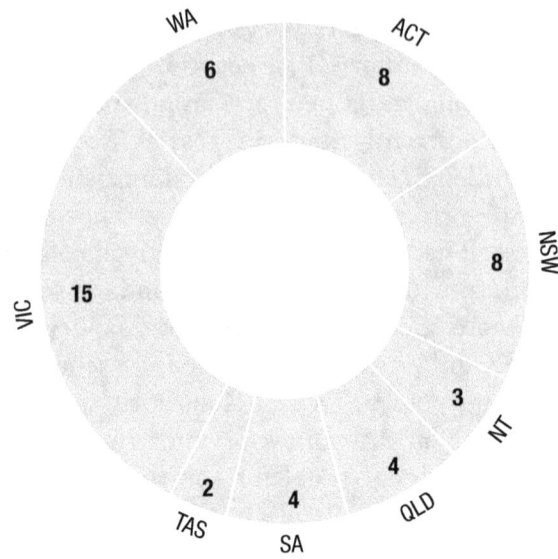

Figure 5.5: Principal participants by state/territory

Figure 5.5 shows the principals' participation by state and territory; as indicated, principals from all states and territories were interviewed. The mix of male and female principals interviewed in each state or territory is showed in Table 5.1.

Table 5.1: Breakdown of principals by state/territory

State	Principals	Female	Male
ACT	8	3	5
NSW	8	3	5
NT	3	2	1
QLD	4	3	1
SA	4	2	2
TAS	2	2	0
VIC	15	3	12
WA	6	3	3
TOTAL	50	21	29

The 50 principals had 910 years of collective teaching experience, representing an average of 18.2 years of teaching per person prior to being appointed as principal of a school.

The female principals collectively had 371 years of teaching experience at the time of the interviews, an average of 17.6 years of experience in the teaching profession prior to principal appointment. Male principals collectively represented 539 years of teaching experience, an average of 18.6 years of teaching experience prior to appointment.

The 21 female principals had totalled 255 years in the principalship at the time interviews took place, an average of 12.1 years overall, while the 29 male principals had a total of 470 years in the principalship, an average of 16.2 years overall, as shown in Figure 5.6. Not all principals offered their age, so we are not able to draw conclusions based on the average age of commencement, but the data suggests that the males were either older on average or were appointed to the principalship earlier in their career than the women. As a complete cohort, the 50 principals had a total of 725 years of experience in the principalship, equating to an overall average of 14.5 years. Thus, the people in the sample group are very experienced teachers and principals.

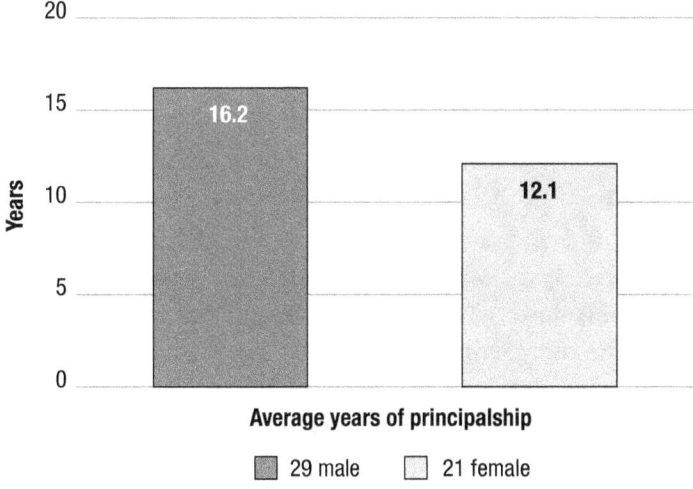

Figure 5.6: Average years of principalship

At the time the interviews took place, the 50 participants had a total of 392 collective years of experience in their current schools, an average of 7.8 years. The 21 female principals had a total of 126 years, at an average of 6.0 years, while the 29 male principals had a total experience in their current school of 266 years, which averages 9.2 years of experience in their current school. Figure 5.7 shows the average number of years of principalship that principals had in their current school.

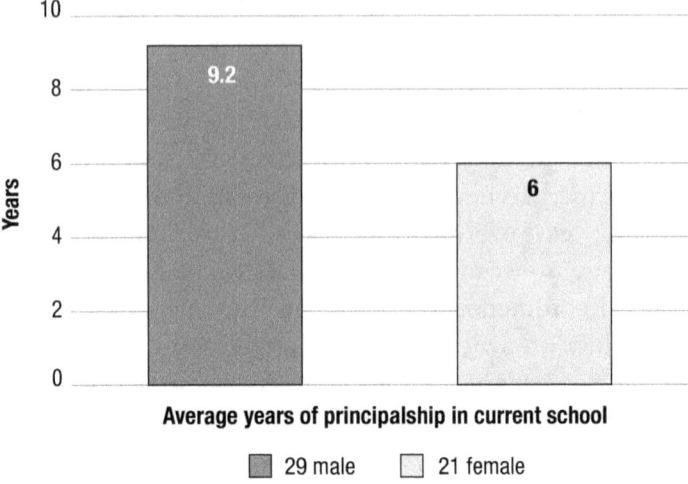

Figure 5.7: Average years of principalship in current school

Conclusion

Overall, the 50 principals who took part in the project are broadly representative in terms of what is a much larger cohort of around 9500 fellow principals across Australia, although secondary principals are somewhat over-represented. Likewise, the principals tended to be more experienced than their peers.

No claims can be made in terms of the overall effectiveness of this group of principals in comparison with their fellow principals, although as researchers and experienced educators we were very impressed with those we had the privilege of engaging with.

Nevertheless, it is hoped that the rich and detailed interviews with these school leaders will provide useful insights into the people who are performing this vital role of school leadership today, and what informs and results from their professional practice.

What follows in Part B are the findings and analysis drawn from the interviews.

PART B

'I'M THE PRINCIPAL' PROJECT FINDINGS

CHAPTER 6
Leading teaching and learning

Introduction
The first four questions of the interview schedule (see Appendix) were devoted to exploring 'Leading Teaching and Learning', one of the five aspects of the 'Professional Practices' outlined in the Australian Professional Standard for Principals. The purpose of these questions, listed by their number below, were to:
1. act as an introductory ice-breaker about participants' motivations to become a principal
2. explore the culture for teaching and learning that principals were attempting to develop
3. ask the principals to reflect on their capabilities for leading teaching and learning
4. enable participants to make further comments about leading teaching and learning.

Motivation to become a principal
In answer to Question 1, 'Tell me about why and what motivated you to become a principal', 9 principals said they found this a 'good' or 'interesting' question.

It was evident from the engagement and tone of responses from the bulk of the principals that the opportunity to reflect and contribute to the study was enjoyable and valuable for them; this question helped participants to clarify and reconsider what was a highly personal and significant professional decision and event.

Most respondents gave a combination of factors rather than a single reason for becoming a principal.

One of the views most commonly expressed was that of their personal values and of wanting to make a difference in improving outcomes for students and their communities. There were comments about having a 'moral purpose' in helping students and teachers to 'flourish', and that they felt they could have a greater impact on student outcomes through being a principal. There were 27 specific responses in this area.

> I wanted to lead change around how schools were run and in particular, each of the schools that I have led had been at a low point, either financially or with morale or community perception or other. It has been my commitment to Catholic education and the story of Catholic education to restore schools and build schools.
> *(Male, Catholic, secondary, metropolitan, ACT)*

> I really enjoyed being in the classroom, but getting into school leadership positions, I think I quickly learned that you can have an impact, a positive impact, on a larger number of students in your community by going into leadership roles … if you want to have the desired impact on a school community, leading teachers and leading leaders is actually the way to do it.
> *(Female, government, secondary, metropolitan, ACT)*

Fourteen principals commented that principals have greater positional power to make change happen more readily and to make a bigger contribution to the school.

> The reason I decided to become a principal was that I thought it would be a profession that offered real leverage to bring about change.
> *(Female, government, secondary, provincial, TAS)*

> I found that my power as teacher, deputy, head of department to make real change was inhibited; being a principal I can really have the license to put in place what I see where education should be at.
> *(Male, government, secondary, metropolitan, WA)*

Sixteen principals spoke of not having an ambition to become a principal initially, but that this developed over time, part of what some termed a 'natural progression'.

> … it was something of a progression in terms of my own personal growth, and learning new information and approaches, and then, ultimately, the step

> into a principal's role ... it's a natural progression to be honest and there was also a sense of, 'I think I could make a difference'.
>
> *(Female, government, senior secondary, provincial, VIC)*

> It was a natural progression once I got into leadership roles. I spent 23 years in a difficult school and looked at the solutions that they were trying to put in place to address the problems in the school; I heard lots of complaints from members of staff and community, and decided I did not want to sit in the back rows and complain. I was better off going into a leadership role and trying to implement the change myself.
>
> *(Male, government, secondary, provincial, NSW)*

Four principals noted how they had become 'bored' with classroom teaching and were looking for greater stimulation and influence.

> It was a developmental thing. I think one of the things I have learned ... is that you reach a point in time in any position where your level of skill, your capability and your awareness of what you are doing, becomes so sophisticated that to keep doing it, almost becomes a little bit monotonous in a strange way, not that you do it with any less passion nor any less diligence, but that you are conscious that you need to do more.
>
> *(Male, government, secondary, metropolitan, NSW)*

Six principals thought they had become better suited to leadership through developing knowledge and skills in schools over time, and that they almost had an obligation to utilise those capabilities.

> I decided to become a principal when I was in the UK. As deputy, I underwent a process run by the National College [for Teaching and Leadership]. It was a national professional qualification for headship. Having undergone that process, and it was quite stringent, I was fairly ambitious and confident in my own ability.
>
> *(Female, government, P–12, metropolitan, ACT)*

> I developed skills, or realised I had skills, that could be better used in the school by taking on smaller leadership roles, or PORs [Positions of Responsibility], and then starting to notice there was probably an opportunity for me to influence others, or do things better, or do things differently.
>
> *(Male, Catholic, P–12, provincial, SA)*

Eight principals said they had 'always' been interested in leadership; they had confidence in themselves to lead and a desire to lead others.

> I have always taken on some form of leadership in a school setting. The biggest reason is I believe I can be most effective by influencing good practice in teachers, sharing my knowledge and helping to coach teachers to become good practitioners; that is the moral purpose as to why I've stepped into that role.
>
> *(Female, government, pre-school–9, remote, NT)*

> Always [had] a strong inner competitive desire to want, to get to this position, when I look back, and I think I know myself really well. Working in the government system, I wasn't prepared to wait to get a more senior position. I wanted it to be based on merit and ability, not on tenure, also a desire to shape a whole school was exciting.
>
> *(Male, independent, primary, metropolitan, NSW)*

On the other hand, there were 9 principals who spoke of negative examples provided by teachers and principals in the sense that these experiences showed them what *not* to do and convinced them that they could do better, rather than just 'sit back' or complain.

> I had a series of frustrating experiences as a teacher and coordinator where I was quite frustrated … with the level of leadership in the school, and I guess I thought … I can do better than that. So, I think it was something I fell into rather than having any great aspirations early on. … I just felt inspired to have a go myself.
>
> *(Male, government, primary, metropolitan, VIC)*

> I felt that I could do it and do it well. I had watched other principals do things that I thought were inappropriate in the area of decision making and the way they used their time … There are not many principals in my experience who gave me any positive role model to follow, it was more looking at them and thinking it shouldn't be done that way, so, to a degree, I built my own model around it.
>
> *(Male, independent, P–12, metropolitan, NSW)*

Four principals spoke of an opportunity arising which they felt they should take up, despite the fact they were not looking for a promotion at the time. An Aboriginal principal noted:

> To become a principal was not something I sought out, in fact, I was quite content being a classroom teacher. I enjoyed the interaction and control in the classroom learning environment you could have, and making a difference in the lives of kids. Other people saw leadership potential in me and pushed me forward. There was an acting position, I needed a job when my husband was transferred, and I was unattached. I said, 'I'll have a go while you find someone else,' and 11 years later ...
> *(Female, government, P–12, very remote, WA)*

Mentors, role models and encouragement to 'step up' were deemed to be important motivators by 18 principals. Some of these principals and others spoke of a desire, and even a sense of duty, to mentor and support others. Women were more likely (n=11) to speak of the influence of – largely female – mentors and role models than men.[111]

> The main motivation was working with wonderful principals. I was unusual for my cohort of teachers, in so far as I had about five female principals I worked for. They developed within me my leadership skills, not really developed, but showed me that I had leadership skills ... I was in my 30s when I became a principal and it was a male-dominated area at the time. It was difficult to be a young female principal.
> *(Female, government, primary, metropolitan, VIC)*

> At the end of secondary schooling I had no idea what I wanted to do. I went to a Year 12 seminar on pathways for Aboriginal students ... for some reason the light bulb went on for me. I went into teaching thinking that my career was to be a teacher forever. In some way, I was guided by school leaders who saw something in me and thought I should be taking the next step.
> *(Male, government, secondary, metropolitan, WA)*

> I had a principal when I was a classroom teacher who identified some potential in me, it started me on a journey of curriculum consultant roles and, after being a deputy for five or six years, I really wanted to step into a principal position, so I had more influence over the bigger picture, the direction of the school, and [to] implement change and take that on myself.
> *(Female, government, primary, remote, WA)*

> I had no intentions of becoming a principal as an early career teacher. I thought that it would be something that I would never, ever want to do, and as, I guess, I went through my teaching career, I happened to stumble

> across an amazing principal of my school, who became a mentor, and by spending time with her, I guess, I learnt how important it was to have people with that strong mix ... we were in a low socio-economic school, so, with a strong sense of social justice, as well as that, you know, educational focus, and what she taught me was around when you're working with students from disadvantage, how important it was to focus on engagement and high standards.
>
> *(Female, government, primary, metropolitan, NSW)*

There were 5 principals who mentioned that they had gone out of schools for an extended period, 2 to corporate roles, 2 in other education positions and 1 teaching overseas, who described this 'time out' as being important in helping them to gain a wider perspective and refocus on what they wanted to achieve. They also mentioned how these other experiences, and the capabilities they developed, were valuable when they became a principal.

> So, my career took me down an interesting path where I remained in education [after leaving schools], I then became a manager of the social justice area in our department, and then, after numerous restructures, I eventually was a manager in curriculum. In some of those roles, my connection with schools was always great because we were always trialling projects in schools, and so my love and passion for schools has never left me, and as a consequence of that ... I had always said that I wanted to finish my career where I started, which was in a school. So, it was always one of my goals to move back into a school.
>
> *(Female, government, primary, metropolitan, QLD)*

> I started as a teacher and moved in to bureaucracy very quickly. Worked in the corporate world then came back to senior executive in the South Australian Department. [I] missed every senior role in schools [and] went from teacher to principal.
>
> *(Male, independent, secondary, metropolitan, SA)*

Another principal described working with Indigenous students for the first time, after more than a decade of teaching, as life-and career-changing, inspiring him to take on the leadership of a largely Indigenous school that 'no one else wanted'.

> I had a varied teaching career, I moved in 1987 into being a teacher at the juvenile justice centre in Adelaide and I worked with offenders between ages of 15–17. In the 22 years of teaching prior to that, I would not have met 22 Aboriginal people. The situation I was in was all Aboriginal children, from all over the state, not just the suburbs of the city, but from remote communities. It sparked my interest in Aboriginal schools. I applied for a job at an Aboriginal school and won it, partly, I think, because some of the people knew of my work in juvenile justice, and also because there was no one else who wanted to do the job. ... I've just loved it [for 14 years]. It wasn't a motivation to be a principal, so much as a motivation to work with Aboriginal people.
>
> *(Male, independent, secondary, very remote, NT)*

Overall, what came through from these principals was a sense of a personal and professional journey of development, and a deepening desire to have a greater impact on teaching, learning and school communities. This was accompanied by a growing sense of capability and duty to make things happen for teachers and students. Other principals had often played a key role in this process of growing capability, confidence and influence.

Developing a culture of teaching for learning

Question 2, relating to the type of culture principals were attempting to create, elicited a wide range of responses, but overall the following key themes or factors emerged:
- the importance and role of personal values and approaches
- having a central focus on teaching and learning
- school ethos
- whole-school approaches
- the role of professional learning
- relationships with students
- leadership development
- teacher appraisal and development
- planning and priorities
- use of research, evidence and data
- school organisation and resources.

In every case, principals reported a strong commitment to students, staff and the community served by the school. This journey was a process of moulding and creating a true learning community with students, and had their welfare and development at the centre; it was accomplished through adherence to the general principles of instructional leadership, despite the contexts of the schools concerned varying widely. The key themes listed earlier are explored below.

The importance and role of personal values and approaches

Principals described their challenge and ambition to improve their school, and to shape its culture. They spoke of the importance of being role models of professionalism, including being seen as a learner. There was a tendency to regard their school as being a large classroom, the importance of them to know every teacher, and to orchestrate teaching and learning. In schools that were staid or 'stuck', principals saw their role as 'disrupting' and reinvigorating. There were comments about driving out defeatism and negativity, and of the challenges of working with experienced, change-averse teachers, regardless of whether the school was low or high performing.

> First of all, I believe it is critical for me to be a leader and having a deep understanding of teaching and learning. We use the terminology of being an instructional leader and that is extremely important for you to have credibility as a principal. I have been around for a long while, been in the classroom, seen good and poor practice, wanting to improve the way that I teach, so it is a real focus on continuing to build our practice. Our focus is on building the collaborative capacity and professional learning through the collaboration.
>
> *(Female, government, pre-school–9, remote, NT)*

> I need to be seen as a learner and insist that the staff around me do the same. We need to constantly develop our teaching and non-teaching staff. They need to take some responsibility for that themselves, if they are truly professionals, they need to have a professional approach to their own growth and development. If you are not learning, you have lost touch with how it feels to be someone in your class.
>
> *(Male, independent, P–12, metropolitan, VIC)*

There was a common view that a new model of more interactive, involved principal leadership was needed and being enacted, despite increasing managerial responsibilities. Principals recognised they couldn't accomplish change and improvement on their own, and that they needed to work with and through other people. Team building, coaching others and gaining consistency were thus considered essential and were advocated by many principals.

> I'm the principal of an early childhood school and I am the founding principal of that school, so it was important that I be really aware, myself, before I began, of what type of culture I wanted to grow, and I think being a new school, I had the opportunity to articulate what I wanted and what my vision of the culture was to teachers who are interested in being appointed in the school ... very much a collaborative culture, where teachers work very much together, where there's an agreement that no one has the right answers, there's an atmosphere and an environment ... [where] we all enquire all the time. We all come together and, in a very collaborative and collegial way, we discuss our practice as a way of making it better and as a way of improving it.
> *(Female, government, early childhood B–8, metropolitan, ACT)*

There was a strong sense of feeling and being responsible for teacher and student learning, development and wellbeing.

> There are some things that I absolutely believe around teaching and learning. One is that there needs to be the conditions for learning to occur – that kids are safe; that there are some expectations in the school and everyone know[s] what they are [to] ensure that those conditions are set, then ensuring that the focus of the decisions we make and the things we put in place are about the students; what impact that has on students – how is it going to help kids progress?
> *(Female, government, secondary, metropolitan, QLD)*

Having a central focus on teaching and learning

Almost half the principals (n=24) spoke of their aim to have a central and consistent school focus on teaching for learning. Some spoke of their school having had a prior focus on student welfare or behaviour that they had attempted to shift or supplant through this stronger focus on teaching and learning. Whole-school use of learning frameworks and theories of action, using the language of pedagogy and instructional leadership were common ways to facilitate this (n=14). Action learning approaches to plan, implement and evaluate change were also mentioned.

> All our staff meetings are focused on professional learning, aligned to what our goals are ... it is about building a coaching and mentoring mindset across the whole school, often using data as a basis and looking at ways they can improve their practice using that data, to get growth in student learning.
> The other thing that is important, is consistency across the whole school. You can get pockets of really good practice, but it is not consistent across the whole school; if you are looking at growth, it needs to be consistent; it is in our plan and becomes an expectation for teachers across the whole school.
> *(Female, government, pre-school–9, remote, NT)*

> We have just been going through our strategic planning process for the next four years and, within that, we are developing an unrelenting focus on learning. We are trying to establish in our vision that schools are a place for learning – in the playground, the community – teachers learning from teachers, teachers learning from students. If you are coming to school, the purpose of coming to school is to learn; that may look different for different kids.
> *(Female, government, P–12, very remote, WA)*

School ethos

Allied to the above focus on teaching and learning, principals spoke of trying to engender a whole-school ethos and culture of reflective practice and continuous improvement; important aspects of this were staff collaboration and planning, and an inclusive culture for students and staff (n=14).[112] There was an expectation that staff 'buying into' this ethos or culture was not optional, but expected. Similarly, there was a strong belief and vision that all students can learn and experience success, and that everyone in the school should be and is a lifelong learner.

> I'm a strong believer that we are a learning organisation, so by nature, being a school, education is our core business, learning is our core business, that should be the same for students as it is for all of us who work in the organisation. I'm an absolute believer in creating a learning organisation where we are all learning, growing our practice, getting a greater understanding of our content areas, a greater understanding of young people and their needs. My role as principal is creating that culture where all of us are on a

> journey of lifelong learning ... teachers, non-teachers, as well as myself and the students.
>
> *(Male, independent, P–12, metropolitan, QLD)*

Also mentioned were people working together in teams, and the notions of collective efficacy and responsibility to create a learning culture that is self-generative and that everyone owns (n=11). A 'coaching culture', where teachers assist their peers through feedback and advice, was also encouraged and implemented in many of the schools. However, there was a corresponding view that while learning opportunities were being provided for staff and students, everyone has a responsibility for their own learning. Similarly, there were comments about the need for a less authoritarian school environment characterised by people taking responsibility for their actions.

The principals recognised that school context was an important aspect of and influence on the ethos and culture they were trying to cultivate.

> What we have been trying to do here is get a culture that honours and respects and values the opinions of Aboriginal people, who are our clientele. We are very remote. They are all Aboriginal parents and communities, and all speak three other languages before English ... Out this way, education is done to Aboriginal people, rather than them being involved in making decisions about direction for the school. My challenge has been to increase the voices of the Anangu people in the everyday running of the school.
>
> *(Male, independent, secondary, very remote, NT)*

Whole-school approaches

Consistent with the above findings, principals (n=13) spoke of the necessity to have whole-school approaches to teacher collaboration, student collaboration in class, and utilising a shared language about teaching and learning. They believed that the curriculum needed to be a school-wide holistic framework and construct, with trans-disciplinary approaches, and congruence vertically and horizontally across all year levels.

> ... you try to develop a school-wide pedagogy, which is really based on the Australian Curriculum capabilities. We want young, enthusiastic, curious learners, who can take risks, collaborate, [and] to look at a myriad of ways to

address a problem. It is about trying to instil in people, 'What do I do when I don't know what to do?', as we live in a world of disruption.

(Female, Catholic, P–12, provincial, SA)

The need for explicit teaching and clear learning intentions across all classes and subjects was also noted. Literacy and numeracy are two areas where whole-school approaches were being implemented, and where teachers had assumed collective responsibility.

> A whole-school approach to literacy and numeracy in terms of creating a timetable and particular structure for these two learning areas to be delivered … Building people's capacity so we have consistency in the types of skills the teachers have in the classroom. So, with writing, we had the whole staff undertake professional learning so there was consistency. Giving teachers some autonomy in the classroom … [Yet] … we were really encouraging them to find the best practice for them, then [for them to] share that with their colleagues.
>
> *(Female, government, primary, remote, WA)*

The role of professional learning

Principals saw professional learning and staff development as crucial to school improvement and being part of core business. There were many comments about making professional learning the focus of staff meetings, and of providing structured opportunities for learning around identified school priorities.

> Pedagogical practices form the basis of 90 minutes of professional learning every Tuesday. The staff meet together for 20 minutes to have an immersion in one of the theories of action we are unpacking … then they have 50 minutes in a professional learning team, which is domain-based, and it is time for an action–research approach, for example, this is the theory of action around using data to inform feedback, 'How am I going to use this in my classroom this week?', or reflect on 'How did I use it last week?' That forms the basis of the professional learning discussions.
>
> *(Female, government, secondary girls, metropolitan, VIC)*

Principals spoke of funding professional learning, sending staff to learn off-site and bringing people to the school to share knowledge.

> We have strong funding; we allocate more than perhaps other schools would in similar [country] areas to professional development. We spend a lot on that; we are happy to send staff to Adelaide even though it is a larger cost. We have staff who need to be released a lot more than others. We prefer them to go face to face if we can, rather than video conference, although sometimes it is unavoidable. We like to think that there is a culture that is pretty well unwritten in some ways; that 'Teaching and learning is the key thing here and what are you going to do about it?'
>
> *(Male, Catholic, P–12, provincial, SA)*

As noted, some schools had structured weekly professional development (PD) sessions or were providing staff with significant blocks of structured PD time in other ways. Some schools had weekend professional learning sessions which, despite being optional, were very well attended. There were comments about 'de-cluttering' staff meetings through reducing administration, and 'housekeeping' to maintain this professional learning focus.

> … we have four Saturday–Sunday conferences every year that are attended by virtually all of the staff. It is voluntary; they don't get time off in lieu or more pay or anything like that. It is linked by a series of teaching and learning workshops about every three weeks after school during the term, so when you start to work out the hours of professional learning time specifically dedicated to this learning … we have all of the normal professional learning on top of that. We go to conferences and events, and goodness knows whatever else, but this was dedicated learning time with our teams themselves, so it speaks volumes about their commitment.
>
> *(Male, government, secondary, metropolitan, NSW)*

The notion that professional learning had two purposes or impacts – collective and individual – was commonly expressed. Trying to develop a coaching culture with peer-to-peer feedback and assistance was also noted by a range of principals. The use of external and internal coaches for areas such as literacy and numeracy was also utilised in some schools (n=5).

Overall, school-wide consistent, collaborative, planned and prioritised professional learning was regarded as an essential driver for school improvement, teacher efficacy and student achievement.

Relationships with students

There were many comments from principals underlining the importance of the relationships between teachers and students. Principals recounted how they were attempting to develop a 'safe', caring, inclusive and accepting environment for all students. Principals spoke of the importance of mutual respect between all within the school, and of the need for students to be fully engaged in school life, which was broader and richer than academic work alone.

> Collaborative culture. There is a broader culture being built around an inclusive and welcoming, respectful community of staff and students, and one of the ways of building that culture is building on relationships between teachers, and between teachers and kids.
>
> *(Male, Catholic, secondary, metropolitan, ACT)*

Providing every student with opportunity and helping each student to develop a 'life pathway' was also mentioned, especially for students in the upper secondary years.

> The last two years of secondary education [is] where young people are making some serious choices about what happens to them in their personal world as well as their potential vocational world ... You need to engage young people in all aspects of the spirit of coming to school. The culture here is one based upon mutual respect. We are all in a learning community where some of us have different roles to play, but we are all committed to helping every single young person to achieve success, by success I mean how we collectively paint a picture of success for each young person. Big challenge. You need to know every student very well and as principal I need to know every teacher well.
>
> *(Male, government, secondary, metropolitan, ACT)*

Leadership development

Principals spoke of the importance and impact of leadership teams, and of developing the leadership capacity of staff in the school. There was common recognition that despite their key leadership role, principals could not accomplish their vision for the school without working with others and delegating responsibility. To that end, trusting, supporting and empowering staff, building instructional leadership capability, coaching, encouraging and mentoring were all noted as being important and powerful agents for change and improvement.

> Our vision for our school is 'success for every student' with a really strong focus on student achievement. We ensure we build our capacity as teachers but also as instructional leaders. Everybody in our leadership team needed to not only see themselves as instructional leaders, but also have the skills to drive the work within our school. We are very systematic that our leadership group had strong coaching and mentoring skills because we saw that as a way to build the capacity of everyone in our organisation.
> *(Male, government, primary, metropolitan, ACT)*

> I suppose the goal here at our school is the distributive leadership culture. So I work really hard at creating teams of people who can facilitate some of that implementation ... generally teachers that are really excited about their curriculum and their pedagogy, and they rise to the opportunity of working with colleagues or working as a team. And so, if someone was to look at the way in which I lead the teaching and learning here at our school, I think they would say it's a distributive model where everyone can be a leader in our school.
> *(Female, government, primary, metropolitan, QLD)*

In some cases, principals spoke of the need to 'rebuild' staff morale, purpose and confidence following difficult periods in the school's history.

> When I first came to this school it was a declining school. It had gone from 850 to 400 kids. Behaviour-wise it was quite bad. [The strategy was to rebuild staff morale, and set high expectations for the kids and the staff, improve the teaching and learning first, then welfare and discipline second.
> *(Male, government, secondary, provincial, NSW)*

Teacher appraisal and development

There were common expressions of the need to 'open up' and 'de-privatise' teaching practice. Principals spoke of opening up classrooms and of the benefits of peer-to-peer collaboration, coaching and feedback. 'Honest' teacher appraisal and feedback were seen as a vital part of this process of changing teachers' views and improving their practice. Some teachers were resistant to observation, appraisal and change, but it was noted that overcoming this was part of the process of changing the culture of the school.

Some principals (n=5) mentioned how they had utilised the Australian Professional Standards for Teachers (APST) to map teacher capability and provide a framework and language for discussions about quality teaching. Some schools had introduced the 'Highly Accomplished' and 'Lead' classifications of the APST as a means of improving teaching and learning, while others had introduced their own school-wide appraisal schemes and frameworks that 'everyone owns'. It was recognised that teacher appraisal methods needed to be both judgemental and developmental. There were comments about teacher appraisal being 'transformative'.

> We developed the performance and development criteria based on the AITSL [i.e. APST] standards. All of my leadership team are qualified cognitive coaches, including myself, and I specifically not mentor, but coach my deputies, and we use the leadership profiles from the AITSL standards as well. Every single teacher knows exactly where they are on the continuum, all of my deputies are assessors, so a lot of professional development has happened, and we have very clear direction so everyone in the school knows what our direction is and ... the expectations of their professional practice.
> *(Female, government, P–10, metropolitan, ACT)*

Some principals provided beginning teachers with reduced teaching loads and mentoring, while others used buddy schemes that paired beginning teachers with more experienced teachers.

Planning and priorities

The importance of having school-wide planning processes that everyone 'bought into', 'owned' and followed was mentioned by many principals. As well as doing all the expected things, the importance of having a small number of key priorities that meshed with student needs and staff professional development, and which would have important spill-over effects on others areas if successful, was noted. Having too many concurrent priorities was seen as problematic in that it diffused effort and made it less likely that these would be successful. Previous failures had, in some cases, resulted in cynical or suspicious staff, and it was important therefore to have some 'wins'.

> In recent times we have had nine strategic planning meetings with staff and we have used a lot of change management processes. [We asked,] 'What motivated you to come into education?', 'What is your moral purpose and why are you here?', 'What is really important to you?' We look[ed] at the common elements then crafted several whole-school statements, which we have now taken to the community, encompassing the values that drive that vision. From there, we look at our school review process, what is it that we are doing well, how can we do it better ... From there, we have particular strategies that we work on as student improvement targets around systemic data and in terms of personalising that.
> *(Female, government, P–12, very remote, WA)*

Use of research, evidence and data

Virtually every principal commented on the value of using evidence or data. Having evidence and using it was seen as key in 'driving' and improving practice and performance; it was viewed as the 'new paradigm' in education.

There were two broad areas from where data were sourced: the data that were already available to the school, which in many cases needed further analysis and 'unpacking', and could be used diagnostically and for planning purposes; and the data the school sought to proactively gather for its own purposes.

In terms of research, there were comments about utilising the work of particular researchers, models or frameworks, in some cases adopted and adapted, and in other cases purchased under licence. Research on learning, effective teaching, leadership and successful schools was used by principals and shared with staff.

> The motivating factor, most recently, has been McKinsey research about leading schools, and leading sectors and countries. It was fascinating and a guiding thing for us over the last three years. It focuses on: the quality of teaching; investing in teacher development; reflection; teams; getting quality teachers; attracting, retaining and developing them; having a healthy curiosity; knowing where you are at; and building in the next stage. The McKinsey report talks about the quality of people and the quality of PD, and having a culture of high expectation that is behind our teaching and learning.
> *(Male, independent, P–12, metropolitan, VIC)*

In terms of gathering data, the use of staff, student and community surveys was mentioned, along with data from observational rounds.

> We have staff surveys that show [a] very strong response to the school's commitment to the professional learning of the teacher. Very strong feedback, [such as,] 'I feel I have an opportunity to grow and improve at the school.' Improved feedback ... 'There are opportunities for me professionally here,' and quite strong feedback ... 'This school values its staff.'
> The other data we have is considerable improvement around growth or beyond expected growth in NAPLAN from Years 7 to 9.
> *(Male, Catholic, secondary, metropolitan, ACT)*

> Key point of reference for us is formative assessment and we use that as a focus for our classroom walk-throughs. Our teams share the formative assessment strategies that they are using and one of the key things that is underpinning that is a culture of trust. They share what they are doing, share the data, plan together, there is a lot of focus on planning, we are testing kids to understand what they can do before they undertake the task, during the task several times, and then at the completion of the task or concept, and reconvening with our kids at different points too. Formative assessment is key here and really skilling people in that space.
> *(Female, government, secondary, provincial, TAS)*

There was a view that data needed to be open to and owned by all. To that end, there were comments from 18 principals about 'data walls', tracking and reporting literacy and numeracy development, common formative and summative assessment tasks, and sharing and using data from these. Being able to measure the impact of various approaches and strategies was seen as essential, although it was acknowledged that there could be problems from gathering 'too much data'.

> One of the ... things I am proud of is that the teacher doesn't see themselves in isolation; they see themselves as responsible for all the students in that year level. So, the data is not about the data from their classroom, it is about the students across the whole year level. There are six or seven teachers in each year level and it is important that they own that data. That allows for co-construction and planning to take place, that is a given here: year levels must collaboratively plan together. It also means that you have moderation across year levels and between year levels.
> *(Male, government, primary, metropolitan, VIC)*

In some cases, principals had commissioned external reviews from bodies such as the Australian Council for Educational Research to provide specialist, objective data and feedback on school performance.

The use of data, evidence and research was recognised as a key aspect of leading and running a school, and of driving change and improvement, which differed from past practices and thinking. It was acknowledged that some staff were threatened by this new paradigm; others, however, had embraced the change and were empowered by the measurable improvements they had been a part of producing.

School organisation and resources

Principals spoke of strategically gathering and utilising the resources available to them. One of the prime resources is, of course, teachers, and a number of principals spoke of careful hiring practices to ensure a good fit with the desired culture and goals of the school. On the other hand, the fact that there were existing staff who were change averse or non-compliant was also mentioned. Some principals spoke of such staff 'moving on' as a result of change or being induced to leave the school, which opened space for more suitable, enthusiastic staff.

> ... during that period of time [of transforming the school] I had a number of older teaching staff members who resigned one by one. So, of the original teachers ... only three remain and they will be here because I want them to be here. They're really good people and they care about the outcomes for children. In the intervening period between then and now, I've been meticulous, well as meticulous as possible, with my selection panels to choose people who were firstly very, very keen [in] seeing children do their best, and could relate to them well and engage with them, and also [we were] looking at their pedagogical knowledge and the way that they operated in their current environment before we employed them.
> *(Male, government, primary, metropolitan, VIC)*

> My best strategy is to hire people who are really, truly smart and clever, much more than what I am, who have a high EQ and know how to manage people.
> *(Female, government, primary, metropolitan, VIC)*

Some principals mentioned recasting formal roles within the school to include new positions such as 'Dean of Students', 'Curriculum Advisor', 'Director of Professional Learning', and 'Director of

Teaching and Learning', along with new groupings of staff such as 'Phases of Learning Teams'. One principal spoke of 'designing the school from scratch [following a fire] around teaching and learning'.

Rewriting and 'de-cluttering' the curriculum and how it was delivered, for example, through vertical student groupings, was also mentioned by some principals. 'Stripping away' the administration and reallocating these resources to supporting teaching and learning was another approach mentioned.

Improving facilities to make them more 'professional' and effective was considered part of the change process by some principals.

Providing more time and opportunity for capacity building within the school day was another strategy noted by principals, particularly in respect of meetings and professional learning, as noted earlier.

Reflection on capabilities for leading teaching and learning

Question 3 on the interview schedule, exploring principals' perceived capabilities and areas of inadequacy, produced responses that were, not surprisingly, largely consistent with the Standard. The data provided were consistent with the five 'Professional Practices' identified in the Standard, as well as data consistent with the three broad 'Leadership Requirements' (see Figure 4.1 on page 39). It was apparent that while there might be a largely common set of overall capabilities required of principals today, as represented by the Standard, the relative strength or weakness of each varied from principal to principal. Thus, for example, while some principals identified curriculum knowledge as an area of strength, others saw the same capability as an area of inadequacy.

Where principals feel most capable

The most commonly reported area of perceived capability was related to people leadership, building teams, coaching, mentoring and building relationships with staff (n=33). Building relationships with students, student welfare, and relationships with parents and the community was mentioned by 10 principals as being an area of capability.

> I think I'm highly capable around building collaborative and strong relationships amongst colleagues and children, and amongst colleagues and parents. I have no doubt that's my strength. I am very much a relational leader.
> *(Female, government, early childhood–8, metropolitan, ACT)*

> [Where I'm] most capable is around human leadership. Issues always arise when you are in an organisation and people bounce off each other. I always try to be firm, but fair and transparent, [and] upfront about how we might solve a problem together and how we go about it. The challenges around human leadership, after the experiences I have had – I feel reasonably confident in.
> *(Female, government, secondary (girls), metropolitan, VIC)*

Their knowledge and understanding of the 'big picture' in education and passing this on to others was noted by more than half of those principals interviewed (n=26) as an area of high capability.

> [I'm] most capable in setting the bigger picture, vision and overall direction, [and] supporting teachers to go in the direction. [I am] focusing my strength now on the 'why'. Why we are doing what we are doing the way we are doing it?
> *(Female, government, primary, remote, WA)*

> I would say my most capable [area] is the big picture, the overview of how curriculum all fits together … And my greatest strength within the national curriculum would be the cross-curriculum priorities. The whole notion of sustainability, cultures [of Aboriginal peoples], Torres Strait Islanders, all that coming through into our units of work as well as the notion of engaging with Asia. I have lots of experience with those three priorities.
> *(Male, government, primary, metropolitan, VIC)*

Personal vision, values and accumulated experience as a teacher and leader were seen as areas of high capability by 23 principals.

> My strength, right through my career, has been understanding of pedagogy, pedagogical processes, neuroscience and all the rest of it. I'm very strong in terms of the capacity to not only talk about quality teaching, but asking hard questions … So, certainly my strength is pedagogical understanding and the leadership of that personally.
> *(Male, government, secondary, metropolitan, NSW)*

CHAPTER 6 : Leading teaching and learning

> I feel in terms of the vision of the school's needs, I am very capable in terms of identifying what we need and initiatives around meeting those needs. I do feel as though I am the leader of ideas in the school, that is a little bit worrying as well as a strength. I think I am a powerful advocate for change to the staff and to the community. I am also very strong in recognising staff and recruiting them into key positions to drive change.
>
> *(Male, Catholic, secondary, metropolitan, ACT)*

Being an effective communicator and sharing knowledge with staff was mentioned by 8 principals. There were comments from 16 principals to do with leading the professional development of staff, and 12 comments to do with principals' own professional learning.

> I feel most capable in being able to work with others to support them, to improve their practice. I learn alongside others. I don't espouse to be an expert in any particular approach or teaching strategies. All professional learning is done side by side with teachers. We do the research together and find out what works best, and my job is to support them to do that to the best of their ability; an enabler, a person who can support them with professional learning and resources; give permission to take risks.
>
> *(Male, government, primary, metropolitan, ACT)*

> I believe that I have a strength of creating a sense of why we need to do things. I am an able communicator. I am able to illustrate to people and develop a message about why we are doing what we are doing; unpack that with my APs to work with staff to make sense of that research. My real strength is my capacity to coach and mentor, and I am quite deliberate about that and the other strength is high care; they only get one shot.
>
> *(Female, government, secondary, provincial, TAS)*

Twenty-two principals considered their areas of high capability to be in the making of: strategic appointments, decision making and problem solving, building the leadership capacities of others, creating new roles, and the strategic use of resources.

> It's become more about being selective and finding, you know, professionals ... our employment processes are virtually looking at an instructional leader position ... I'm shortlisting now and making sure that the people that are coming into those roles have really good experience in the shoulder-to-

> shoulder support because I find that all the additional activities that I've got on my plate now don't allow me in the classroom as much.
> *(Female, government, primary, metropolitan, NSW)*

> I feel most capable about leading learning for teaching. [I] have done a lot of PD around leading direct instruction. [I am] very confident around assessment for, and of learning – using the data to demonstrate the detail in that, using IT to facilitate that, using my senior staff around me to support that. I have changed the leadership structure to enable me to do that.
> *(Male, Catholic, primary, provincial, VIC)*

Eighteen principals saw knowledge of research, involvement in research, and the use of evidence and data for monitoring and improvement as an area of capability.

> I certainly believe I have a very sound intellectual understanding – a professional understanding about what the world of research is saying around outstanding learning and teaching generally, but also in the senior secondary sense. I also believe I have a strong capacity within the notion of being able to share that knowledge with others, whether it be my peers in the local network of schools, peers across the ACT or further afield.
> *(Male, government, secondary, metropolitan, ACT)*

> Most capable ... I guess ... monitoring and reporting on student achievement. I'm certainly very capable in that. Analysing data – very capable in that – and feeding that back to staff and community.
> *(Female, government, primary, provincial, NSW)*

Eleven principals saw contributing to creating an overall school culture to support teaching and learning as a strength.

> The development of culture within an open-door policy has worked to my advantage. The more you are in principalship, the less you are likely to have intimate knowledge of the six KLAs. I delegate, but there is no doubt I had a much more articulate knowledge when I was teaching. I do try to attend every PD meeting in relation to curriculum; Hattie's research is making sure principals are in attendance. I also make sure that I don't miss any development days that my staff may have.
> *(Male, independent, primary, metropolitan, NSW)*

Where principals feel least adequate

Overall, principals showed a high level of awareness that the role of being a principal was increasingly about being an instructional leader.

There were 16 principals who commented that they found it difficult to be an instructional leader due to the managerial pressures of running a school, and 9 principals spoke of the 'distractions' posed by 'paperwork' and keeping up with mandated change. Not having sufficient time for 'core business' was also a common regret.

> I feel most inadequate in getting the time to spend on [curriculum] ... it is a full-time role. If that is the only thing we had to do, we would still be challenged by that. It is an enormous task and schools are the last opportunity in our world where students are in a hopeful, secure place to work with teachers on learning and through learning, and we must privilege that. I feel that it does not get enough of my attention.
> *(Female, Catholic, P–12, provincial, SA)*

> My least [capability] is doing the administrative side of my job. There is so much that takes me away from the classroom. There is a lot of management of a small business rather than running a school. Sometimes I feel I am not holding up my part of the bargain in being visible ... I'd like to be more strategic and more targeted in how I use my time in the classroom for helping teachers and students.
> *(Female, government, primary, metropolitan, WA)*

> My weakness in managing a school and getting caught up in the day-to-day operations means that you don't always give it the time and place that it deserves for improving; things don't just stop because you're out doing observations.
> *(Female, government, P–12, very remote, WA)*

One of the other major areas of reported inadequacy was in feeling removed from classrooms, and not being 'visible' and able to work with teachers individually. This was allied to a feeling of being out of touch with current teaching practice as some principals (n=10) had left classroom teaching some time ago.

> I have been out of the classroom for 10 years, so I feel that this is where my weakness is. I am feeling removed from that.
> *(Female, government, primary, remote, WA)*

> The area I feel out of my depth in is knowing whether it happens in the coalface [where the work happens], once the doors are shut … That is where you probably feel inadequate. You can talk the talk, but you don't get the opportunity as the principal to walk the walk in the classroom; that is up to the teacher.
>
> *(Male, Catholic, P–12, provincial, SA)*

Keeping up to date with curriculum changes and developing and evaluating curricula was of concern to 14 principals. Some of these principals commented that they had become 'out of touch' and had to leave curriculum leadership to others.

> Where I feel less skilled is in the new curriculum because sitting in my seat, in a school my size, I find it difficult to get down to the teaching and learning, and knowing the curriculum like I used to. I used to be very knowledgeable in curriculum, however, the demands in this position have almost flooded over the top of me, and that is why I have put in place a second AP to assist in that area because I knew that my skills … were not as good as they should be.
>
> *(Female, government, primary, metropolitan, VIC)*

Aspects of work pressure were noted by 10 principals; they spoke of being a poor model to others of work–life balance, of problems in keeping up to date with their own professional learning, and a lack of time in general due to their role.

> I understand I don't have the same capacity to undertake the research and phenomenal amount of reading that I used to do. Leading the school, and the amount of paperwork the department requires, takes away some of my time to stay abreast of the current research. Despite that, we lead action research teams here every year and try to stay on top of what research is telling us about how to do things better. Probably not doing those things as sharply as I did before … Maybe I have high expectations of myself to stay abreast of all of those things.
>
> *(Female, government, secondary, provincial, TAS)*

> I am probably not a great example of work–life balance, even though I talk about that with everybody else. An area of need that has diminished over the years has been around personalising the things that happen too much. Certainly as a young leader, it is hard not to take a lot of criticism personally,

> or a lot of things that occur that you just sort of internalise probably a lot more than you should.
> *(Male, government, secondary, metropolitan, NSW)*

Using evidence and data and assisting other staff to do so was mentioned as an area of perceived inadequacy by 7 principals.

> [An] area for improvement is definitely around understanding effect size and data. I can see the general picture quite readily, but I need to get better at the technicality of understanding what the data is telling me, and therefore what to put into the improvement plan for cohorts of students or individual students. That is where I feel less adequate, around the technical skill of data analysis.
> *(Female, government, secondary (girls), metropolitan, VIC)*

Dealing with difficult people and underperforming staff was mentioned as problematic by 10 principals.

> The most challenging part is when you have poor performance. I make assumptions sometimes that teachers know stuff and then I have to take a backward step sometimes when they don't ... What happens when you have a teacher, when they have mindset that they don't need to improve? Even when you pull out the data ... We have performance improvement plans, and they take a lot of time and energy.
> *(Female, government, preschool–9, remote, NT)*

> My weakest area would be in difficult conversations. I hate having unpleasant conversations with people and so if I've got a teacher who's underperforming or a parent who's angry ... I don't mind the kids so much, but difficult conversations with adults are painful and I postpone them sometimes, which is a weak thing to do.
> *(Male, independent, P–12, provincial, VIC)*

Other issues about leading teaching and learning

The optional question asking about other comments concerning teaching and learning drew lengthy responses from 41 of the 50 principals. Often such answers proved insightful as respondents' deeper thinking had been facilitated by previous questions.

There was an eclectic selection of additional remarks and issues, but also some strong commonalities. Selective recruiting, developing, and working with the senior leadership team of the school was seen to be important by 17 principals. There were comments about trusting the senior leadership team, distributing leadership and empowering people to 'get on with it'.

> The conversations you have with the high-level leadership team in your school is really important as you can draw on the wisdom, knowledge and expertise of others. The construct of your leadership team is really important in ensuring that you keep moving things forward and building the capacity of your teachers too.
> *(Male, government, secondary, metropolitan, VIC)*

There were 14 comments from principals who were striving to create the conditions and culture in their school for teaching and learning, despite the fact they were not directly involved in classrooms.

> ... the role of the principal, I think, has kind of really moved away from being able to be a hands-on leader of teaching and learning, and really has become more about, you know, being knowledgeable about what's out there and, you know, you really need to know your context and your staff to be able to facilitate that.
> *(Female, government, primary, metropolitan, NSW)*

> It is about creating the environment where staff feel secure to have a go and feel supported, and, critically, that they feel they have been listened to. I have had to hold the line on some things, but if people can come to me with a reasonable line of enquiry, then I am open to change. It's about getting people involved in the discussion and the process.
> *(Male, government, K–10, metropolitan, WA)*

A common concern was to do with maintaining focus on the core business of leading learning and teaching in the face of mandatory accountability and managerial responsibilities. Eight principals mentioned the difficulty of finding enough time to devote to learning and teaching in their school.

> It is always a juggling act between knowing it is the core business of what we are doing, yet often the principal and the deputies find that their time and focus is taken up with other things, whether it is OHS, staff issues, hiring. You meet a parent down the street and all they are interested in is whether

> their child is learning how to read and write properly, and I know that most of my day has been chewed up with meetings about finance, OHS, union negotiations, hiring, with staff, meetings with the council about trying to build a new fence on a different property.
>
> *(Male, Catholic, P–12, provincial, SA)*

> System wide, and I speak to colleagues about this all the time, principals really want to be instructional leaders and leaders of learning. It is a continuing frustration for principals ... the time spent doing other peripheral tasks that are somewhat erroneous are eating into their time.
>
> *(Male, government, primary, metropolitan, ACT)*

Principals spoke of their need for continual professional learning (n=4) and how they had tried to raise the general standard of teaching and learning in the school through professional development and professional sharing of expertise (n=8).

The range of challenges mentioned by the principals included dealing with under-performing staff, moving away from summative examinations to measuring 'what matters most', increased accountability which is not about 'core business', the difficulty of communication in a large school, not using student voice feedback sufficiently, finding the right instruments and data to measure success, getting everyone on board to enable whole-school approaches, the temptation to keep doing the same things that aren't working, finding ways to bring the school together, and keeping up with curriculum change.

Conclusion

Overall, what came through from the interview responses to the questions devoted to exploring 'Leading Teaching and Learning' was the strong desire expressed by most of the principals to be an effective instructional leader, and to put teaching and learning at the centre of the school, despite ongoing difficulties and distractions. The vast majority of responses communicated a strong sense of passion, enthusiasm, and commitment to people and the improvement of their school.

CHAPTER 7
Developing self and others

Introduction
Questions 5 to 13 of the interview schedule (see Appendix) were devoted to exploring 'Developing Self and Others', one of five aspects of the 'Professional Practices' outlined in the Australian Professional Standard for Principals. The purpose of these nine questions, listed below by their number in the schedule, was to ask the principals to:
  5. outline important qualities of being a good principal
  6. reflect on the main contributors and influences on their present capabilities
  7. outline the knowledge and skills they believed assist them most in their role
  8. reflect on how they believe others within and outside the school saw them as a principal
  9. give their views on professional learning and development of self and others
  10. comment on the role they believe principals should play in professional development of others and the strategies they personally employ
  11. assess their state of wellbeing
  12. assess the current state of wellbeing of their staff
  13. make further comments about developing self and others in their school.

Qualities of a good principal
Question 5 asked principals to consider what they believed were important qualities of being a good school principal. It sparked a range of responses including the need for strong interpersonal and intrapersonal skills, and key personal qualities and values were highlighted. Featured prominently were comments about building strong relationships, knowing staff, students and the broader community, and being an active listener. Of the 50 principals interviewed, 21 commented on the need for strong interpersonal

skills. These skills, as a leader, were imperative to 'building a collective vision', 'influencing others' and 'creating change'. While 15 principals commented on the need for principals to have the technical skills and competencies to 'stay on top of school operations' and 'manage their time', the importance of the relational aspects of the job were considered paramount.

Understanding and dealing with people

> The EQ [emotional intelligence] stuff – how you manage and deal with people, how well you can listen and decipher what they are really on about – you need technical knowledge and you can't be a fool, but the EQ stuff is far more important than the IQ stuff.
> *(Male, independent, P–12, metropolitan, VIC)*

> Interpersonal skills – that is the number one. People can be technically brilliant, but a disaster as part of their community because it is a heart-and-mind job. You have to be caring for every student in your school and every adult who works in your community.
> *(Male, government, secondary, metropolitan, VIC)*

Interpersonal skills

The 21 principals who mentioned the importance of interpersonal skills commented on the need for principals to communicate ideas, listen, be empathetic, engage in difficult conversations, and work effectively with others. Developing relationships with all stakeholders was also considered an integral part of the principal role.

> It is a little bit like what it is for teachers. It is around relationships, respect and rigour. It is really important that principals can build terrific relationships with their staff, students and community.
> *(Female, government, secondary, provincial, TAS)*

> I think you've got to have good interpersonal skills, and you have to be genuine in your interactions with people.
> *(Female, government, primary, provincial, NSW)*

> I do think that you do need to have good strong interpersonal skills so that you can actually relate and empathise with other people.
>
> *(Female, government, preschool–primary, metropolitan, NT)*

Authenticity and knowing oneself

Thirteen principals spoke of the importance of being 'authentic' and 'credible'. These comments built on others about needing to develop professional and relational trust, being transparent and displaying integrity. Some principals mentioned that being authentic came from a well-developed understanding of self, underpinned by personal and educational values, hard work, and a commitment and care to develop others.

> You have got to be in it for the right reasons – very genuine and authentic. It flows over to how you come across to staff and parents, and students as well.
>
> *(Male, Catholic, P–12, provincial, SA)*

> Build a beautiful rapport with children; getting them to feel that you genuinely care for them, same for the staff; they want you to be interested in them; to show that you genuinely care for them, and their development and growth as an educator.
>
> *(Male, government, primary, metropolitan, VIC)*

> Understand who you are. I joke at myself and this is about me keeping it real. Not taking yourself too seriously, but it is more than that. Understanding and being real about what your keys skills are and what [they] aren't. Be authentic to that. Don't try and convince the other senior people that I am anything but that.
>
> *(Male, independent, P–12, metropolitan, VIC)*

> In my own context, I think it is necessary to have a spiritual strength, consistency between the ethos of the school and my own personal ethos … I can't lead unless I'm authentic to myself.
>
> *(Female, Catholic, secondary, metropolitan, QLD)*

The ability to know one's strengths and weaknesses, and to consider the needs of the school, were considered necessary in building a team and getting the right people for the job.

> You are the leader. I know that I am not the expert in quite a number of areas. It takes a fair bit of humility to acknowledge that you don't have to be and to support others in their areas of growth, and step back and get out of their way, and allow them to do their job.
>
> *(Male, independent, P–12, metropolitan, QLD)*

> One of the most important qualities is the ability to know yourself, know what your strengths and weaknesses are, understand those and determine whether you are going to [reduce] those weaknesses or employ people to fill those gaps.
>
> *(Male, independent, P–12, metropolitan, QLD)*

Developing and working others

Twenty-one principals spoke specifically of developing others. This included 'supporting people to be lifelong learners', mentoring aspiring leaders and 'giving them opportunities to lead'. Some principals in smaller and remote schools acknowledged that building a team and supporting the development of new leaders was more difficult.

> I think some of the most important qualities would be around that capacity to build others as leaders.
>
> *(Female, government, secondary, metropolitan, ACT)*

> I've had a number of staff leave here, and go and get principal jobs or assistant principal jobs, or leading teacher jobs elsewhere, and I'm always happy when that occurs, even though I don't like losing good people. It shows me that we're having an impact on the leadership qualities of the people who work for this organisation, and to me that's absolutely critical.
>
> *(Male, government, primary, metropolitan, VIC)*

> That is really important, you need to identify future leaders and build the succession planning within, in my case, the state system, so we have good state system leaders coming through.
>
> *(Female, government, secondary girls, metropolitan, VIC)*

Six principals commented on the importance of having a sense of humour and 'not taking yourself too seriously'. A passion for 'what you are doing' and for young people was mentioned by 7 principals, while 6 commented on the need to be resilient, to have 'mental toughness' and a 'very thick skin'.

> If staff get upset and have a go at me, I don't take it personally. Everyone gets frustrated; we are human beings. If a parent gets angry, I always thank them for coming in and [for] showing ... passion about their child's education. That shows they care.
>
> *(Male, government, K–10, metropolitan, WA)*

Overall, an understanding of self and others came through as important perceived qualities of good principals. Being able to work with and through others, and having the confidence and vision to lead a school, while managing the operational and relational demands, were also considered imperative to being a good school principal.

Influences on capabilities and knowledge and skills required in the role

Questions 6 and 7 asked principals to reflect on the main contributors and influences on their present capabilities, and to outline the knowledge and skills they believed assisted them most in their role.

The influence of others

Twelve principals mentioned the influence of others on their present capabilities. They commented on people who saw potential in them earlier in their career, and of being encouraged and provided with leadership opportunities. Nineteen commented on the influence of observing others, both the 'good' and 'bad', as having a significant influence on how they lead.

> What I did very carefully within all leadership roles, and as a classroom teacher, was to watch and learn and listen – to learn about what good leadership looked like and what it didn't look like.
>
> *(Male, government, primary, metropolitan, ACT)*

Important experiences

Fourteen principals spoke of the importance of reflection, learning from experience and mistakes.

> I've learnt to do that via experience. I'm certainly a different leader after 15 years as a principal than what I was after two years as a principal. A lot of it's experience and learning by your mistakes, and also realising that there's more than one way of doing things.
>
> *(Female, government, primary, metropolitan, VIC)*

Thirteen principals commented that their career experiences outside schools had supported the development of their capabilities and breadth of experience.

> I was on the AITSL Foundation Board when we were developing the teacher standards and principal standard. The people on the board had a wealth of experience in education, and had other perspectives on how things could be managed. I also [worked] on how Indigenous funding gets allocated to improving and closing the gap; looking at policy influence and how it impacts on the ground is quite powerful as well.
>
> *(Female, government, P–12, very remote, WA)*

> Outside of teaching, I had a successful career as an AFL umpire and some leadership roles there as secretary of a large association. So, I guess it was not just one thing, but a range of experiences that enabled me to understand what whole-school leadership was all about.
>
> *(Male, government, secondary, metropolitan, VIC)*

Mentoring, professional learning and networks

Mentoring (n=31), professional learning (n=25), and trusted colleagues and professional networks (n=21) featured predominantly as significant contributors and influences on present capabilities of the majority of the principals. Some mentioned having an informal mentor in the education sector, while others commented on mentors from elsewhere as influencing their capabilities. Some principals mentioned role models in their family, while others spoke of their family and upbringing in shaping their current capabilities.

> I enjoy my conversations with [a fellow principal], maybe more than I do with others because he will come in and ask, 'Why are you doing it this way?' I call on him as a mentor, the good thing about his stuff is that if I haven't made contact for a few days, he will just drop me a line and say, 'Are you ok; need help with anything?' The relationship stuff with others has contributed to who I am today.
>
> *(Male, independent, secondary, very remote, NT)*

Professional learning was considered an influence and contributing factor to present capabilities, knowledge and understandings of principals. Twenty-five principals commented on how formal and informal professional learning had influenced their capabilities by 'applying the theory and learning'; formal and informal professional learning was also acknowledged as assisting principals in the development of their knowledge and skills in Question 7. Others spoke of continued learning to build their knowledge and understanding. Some mentioned formal learning through courses and programs, and other principals mentioned more informal approaches, such as reading, engaging in social media, and visiting other schools and systems. A subset of this group mentioned knowledge about change management and drawing on leadership models assisted them in better understanding their role as a leader.

> Keeping our finger on that pulse is important, but making sure that we're not leaping and jumping, that we actually are assessing things and working out what is critical or what is going to work for our context in our situation.
>
> *(Female, government, secondary, metropolitan, ACT)*

> The basic skill base and knowledge base is important. I top it up through social media and my own personal learning network. That's my reading now.
>
> *(Male, independent, P–12, metropolitan, VIC)*

> I am aware of many frameworks, learning frameworks and whole-school change frameworks that shape my own theories and understanding of how things happen.
>
> *(Female, Catholic, primary, metropolitan, SA)*

Understanding people

Twenty-seven principals commented on the importance of principals having an understanding of people and 'people skills'. A knowledge of their community, staff strengths and weaknesses, being able to 'read' people, empathise and bring people on board were commented on as important understandings in their role as a principal.

> Knowledge about people and working with people, without doubt … is the most important stuff a principal can have. If you don't know how to relate to people – how people learn, how people are different – you can't go to the next step.
>
> *(Male, government, secondary, metropolitan, WA)*

A knowledge of 'how people learn' and a 'good foundational understanding of teaching and learning' was considered an important capability and was mentioned by 22 principals.

> A lot of conversation at the moment [is] that principals need a deep pedagogical knowledge, and I think they do – understanding what good learning is about. Sometimes I worry about not having been in the classroom for so long. It is important today if you want to move your school, and move your students along [to know] what is and isn't effective.
>
> *(Female, government, secondary, metropolitan, QLD)*

Knowledge of school operations

A knowledge of school operations and processes was mentioned by 19 principals as important for managing the school.

> I think for the role of principal, to maintain the harmony in our schools to the best of our ability, the technical leadership is critical.
>
> *(Male, independent, P–12, metropolitan, VIC)*

> What assists me most is that I believe I've got a good broad knowledge and understanding of what is going on, I am not too aloof in some areas, am not bluffing my way through, but I can talk to every single person and have a little bit of knowledge about every single thing that is happening across the school.
>
> *(Male, Catholic, P–12, provincial, SA)*

While acknowledging the need for skills in managing school operations, many commented that this wasn't the only understanding required.

> I have a broad-brush understanding of all those pieces of legislation, curriculum documentation – stuff that you need to have a bit of an understanding of to run a school, but if you immersed yourself in this and had a deep understanding of every piece of legislation there is, you would be forever buried at your desk, and then you are becoming the expert in those areas. [You are] ignoring the fact that you actually need to lead people and unlock their potential, and create a learning organisation.
> *(Male, independent, P–12, metropolitan, QLD)*

A wider perspective

Twelve principals commented on the importance of principals having a knowledge of the wider world. This included local, national and global contexts, and an understanding of the cultures that make up their community.

> In my role, my collective experience and understanding of three completely different Aboriginal cultures is the most important bit of knowledge that I have; it is not always obvious knowledge, but it affects the way I operate.
> *(Male, independent, secondary, very remote, NT)*

> Knowledge and understanding? I think ... just awareness of societal trends, and an awareness of sociology and psychology; really, the way groups are evolving and the way individuals are evolving, and how we can be at the forefront in helping that evolution go in a healthy direction. Schools seem, these days, to be tagging along well behind society, and trying, kind of earnestly, to please everyone and to keep up with what society is doing and to meet every demand.
> *(Male, independent, P–12, provincial, VIC)*

This section of wider world knowledge elaborated on a subsection in Chapter 6, which considered the aspects that motivated principals to become leaders. As in that chapter, many principals spoke of their current capabilities stemming from previous experiences, observing how others lead, and acknowledging people who saw potential in them and offered them opportunities. Embedded approaches to professional learning were highlighted by many principals, while most acknowledged professional learning as contributing to their current capabilities, and assisting with their understanding and knowledge.

Perceptions of you as a leader

Question 8 asked principals to consider how people within and outside their school saw them as a leader. This provided an opportunity for principals to reflect on their role and the perceptions others had of their capabilities.

When the principals were asked about how others saw them as a leader, they mostly mentioned: 'being approachable' (n=21); 'having high expectations' and 'being determined and relentless' (n=21); 'having high regard' and 'respect from others' (n=17); and 'being genuine' (n=16).

Being seen as approachable, accessible

To be approachable included being available for students, parents and staff, and being supportive; some principals (n=4) spoke of being considered a 'problem solver' people could go to.

> Competent, approachable, that the door is open. Students come quite freely to talk to me about things – issues as well as good things. Parents are quite open about contacting me directly if they need to. I think approachable and professional, I hope, is how they see me.
> *(Female, government, secondary girls, metropolitan, VIC)*

> I think they see me as being approachable. People do recognise that I am easy to talk to. I don't live in an ivory tower and I have a fairly open door. Problem solver. I try to work through problems and come up with the best solutions with people.
> *(Female, government, preschool–9, remote, NT)*

While being approachable was seen as important, others commented on the challenges of being accessible. This was noted especially by principals in larger schools.

> I think sometimes people find it a bit frustrating that they can't get to see me. I have had an open-door policy; they are very good. I try to make myself accessible, up to 18 meetings a week.
> *(Male, independent, P–12, metropolitan, VIC)*

Some spoke about distributed leadership assisting with maintaining a sense of accessibility.

> Some staff might think I am remote, but that could be a misunderstanding of how big the role is, and that they are just one of 400 permanent staff. I can't do the direct one-on-one classroom visits and observations. I have to make sure their teams do that.
> *(Male, independent, P–12, metropolitan, VIC)*

> I have lots of mini interactions with students and parents. I would hate for everything to come to me – hate to micromanage basically – you can't get a yes/no answer because you have to run it past a very controlling principal. Decentralised decision making. My mobile number is freely available to students and staff. Problems do get sorted out before they get to me, but they know if there is an answer that is not fair they can still come to me.
> *(Male, government, secondary, metropolitan, VIC)*

Being seen as having high expectations, respected, genuine

Twenty-one principals commented that people see them as having high expectations of themselves and others. Some principals commented that others saw them as 'relentless' and 'determined' when challenging other people's behaviours and expectations.

> Last year I had to go through a process with two teachers. Ended up having to manage two teachers out of the school; it was a stressful time. People and the community realise that if [teachers] are underperforming they are going to be challenged. The parents, staff and students saw that we take action against it, and we did it in a dignified way.
> *(Male, Catholic, primary, provincial, VIC)*

> I am a stickler for things. I follow policy admin procedure to the letter. People acknowledge the high standards I set for myself, but also that I achieve them. I have high standards for others I work with and reaching the goals that we set, but also having empathy ... we support people.
>
> *(Female, government, hospital school, metropolitan, NSW)*

Seventeen principals commented on people having respect for them and of being held in high regard.

> I'm respected in the community for other things as well. I'm sensible and asked to do a number of things in the community. [I] chair a panel at the council.
>
> *(Male, Catholic, P–12, provincial, SA)*

> More recently as we are now delivering on the strategic plan, [there is] a great deal of respect and admiration for what is being achieved.
>
> *(Male, independent, P–12, metropolitan, VIC)*

Sixteen principals made comments on being perceived as 'genuine' and being known for making decisions based on the best interest of students.

> I think I would be seen as someone who is fair and looks at the interest of students first when making my decisions. I think most parents would see me that way.
>
> *(Male, government, secondary, metropolitan, VIC)*

Gaps in perceptions

Some principals acknowledged a difference between their perception of how others see them and how they see themselves. Many principals referred to evidence in supporting their interpretation. They mentioned the use of surveys, 360-degree feedback tools and anecdotal comments, while others acknowledged that it depended on the role they were in and who you were talking to as to how they were perceived.

> There are bound to be people who see me as being headstrong. Many who see me as being visionary. Many who see me as innovative, but they don't

> know what I've done. People see you through the lenses they want to see you through.
>
> *(Male, independent, P–12, metropolitan, NSW)*

While many commented on the positive perception others had of them as principals, 7 spoke of not always being liked and acknowledged, and that leading change and challenging others meant all people did not like you all the time.

> I think ... depending on [the] stage of the journey that you're at ... with your bringing in change that people will view me as, certainly, passionate, but that sometimes it feels too fast or it's too many ideas ... I'm a change maker, but then what I've always found is that by persevering and continuing to be really explicit about what you're doing that you're able to bring most people on board.
>
> *(Female, government, preschool and primary, metropolitan, NT)*

> Principals cannot expect everyone to like them and they have to come to terms with that. You are always going to have people who for any number of reasons will have an issue with something. You have to keep your head around what is the best for the majority – the common good.
>
> *(Male, government, primary, metropolitan, VIC)*

Professional learning, and the role of the principal in the development of self and others

For Questions 9 and 10 of the interview schedule, respectively, each principal was asked, 'What is your view on professional learning and development of self and others?' and, 'What role should a principal play in the professional development of others?' Continuing on from comments made in Chapter 6 around the culture principals were developing for teaching and learning in their schools, these questions sought to find out more about the professional practice of developing self and others.

The importance of professional learning

As in Chapter 6, the importance of professional learning was acknowledged by principals. Principals used words such as 'critical', 'pivotal', 'vital' and 'fundamental' when explaining the importance of professional learning for school improvement and the development of self and others. Some mentioned the need for themselves and others to be 'lifelong learners', and to keep up to date with new knowledge and understandings, while others commented on continuous professional learning being part of their and their staff's obligatory duties as professionals.

> It is a priority, it has to be. We live in such a dynamic environment, not only within schools, but the whole global system, so we need to be constantly learning about how to adjust to that.
> *(Female, government, primary, remote, WA)*

> Absolutely intrinsic to being a professional educator. Gone are the days when your degree from 1975 will serve you well for 40 years. When I entered the profession that was very much the attitude, and there may still be some who have managed not to invest in contemporary professional learning to adapt their skills and capacity. If you are a doctor and you haven't invested in any professional learning since 1975, I don't want you to go anywhere near me, so why don't we do that in our profession?
> *(Male, government, secondary, metropolitan, ACT)*

> I consider it imperative, if we are being paid as professionals we need to respond as professionals. Being engaged in ongoing professional learning is critical, and I need to ensure our school has a robust and rigorous program of professional learning as well as enabling our staff to access professional learning outside of the school, around their own personal identified goals, identified goals for their professional learning plan or in line with school priorities.
> *(Female, government, secondary, provincial, TAS)*

Being a lead learner

Most principals (n=29) commented on their role as a 'lead learner'. Principals commented on the importance of being involved in the learning, setting a symbolic 'message' of its value, and 'taking a lead in discerning and prioritising whole-school professional learning'.

> My role is that if we are doing anything in-house, I am there. I hear it the same as the teachers. I need to show my teachers that I value the time we are spending. I am not called away. My office has to handle any concerns

> or take messages. I have to be there the whole time, so I send a very strong message that I value what is occurring.
>
> *(Female, government, primary, metropolitan, VIC)*

> That you are actually involved in the conversations and the PD that is happening – that symbolic stuff is pretty important as it sends a message that you value the learning.
>
> *(Male, government, secondary, metropolitan, VIC)*

> I think it is important that the principal supports that professional learning. And even if the principal is not an expert, if you are not interested, people don't see that it is valued. It is important that it is valued.
>
> *(Female, Catholic, primary, metropolitan, SA)*

Some principals did comment, however, on how the demands of the job made their involvement in professional learning more difficult.

> Becoming harder and harder – [the] principal should be the lead learner and facilitating opportunities for staff. Our program is significantly impacted next year with OHS, child safety, fire management. All those things need to come into our schedule, and you have to be responsive to staff needs as well, so mid-term we build-in a no-meeting schedule and if there is a parent interview night, we take up one of the professional development days.
>
> *(Male, Catholic, primary, provincial, VIC)*

> I find I'm probably not doing as much professional leading as I was four or five years ago. I find it increasingly hard to do that. The demands of the job in a range of ways seem to have escalated, and so there are times when I've had patches, months at a time where I look back and think I haven't actually done anything for myself in terms of professional growth or development. I've been doing the transactional stuff and the in-school leadership stuff, but I haven't looked for opportunities for myself.
>
> *(Male, government, senior secondary, provincial, VIC)*

Fostering a culture of learning

Most principals said their key role was setting up the structures and processes to enable learning, allocating financial and human resources, and being responsible for setting-up a culture of learning.

> I think resourcing is one of the most important things, and I'm not talking about resourcing professional learning courses, I'm talking about resourcing things like collaborative learning, lesson studies, planning programming development. I'm talking about identifying areas within the school based on student need to build student learning success, that ... and then sourcing the kind of professional development that's going to best build that capacity in teachers.
>
> *(Female, government, primary, provincial, NSW)*

> The other part is creating the time and the resources that are necessary to support people to learn and to grow; constantly seeing what time you can find; how you can do it; what people you can get to help; are there other organisations who can assist and communicating stuff back and forth.
>
> *(Male, government, secondary, metropolitan, VIC)*

> The role of the principal is about a team. I provide the structures and consultation that enable professional learning to be a part of the narrative of the work of the school.
>
> *(Male, government, secondary, metropolitan, ACT)*

> Creating a culture where that is acceptable. No matter what area you are looking at, my role is strategic. I put processes in place, creating a climate of trust, where people are not afraid to take risks – a climate of respect.
>
> *(Female, government, primary, metropolitan, WA)*

Aligning professional learning with school goals and priorities

Many principals spoke of the importance of alignment between professional learning, and school goals and priorities, commenting on the importance of professional learning that was 'job-embedded', 'in context', focused on 'what I need to learn', and taking an 'action-learning', 'evidence-based' and 'problem-based' approach.

> Best professional learning happens in schools when teachers identify a problem of practice, and together ... work at developing a theory of action, implementation and monitoring impact.
>
> *(Female, government, secondary, provincial, TAS)*

> We need to be very attuned to our core purpose and the main goals we are trying to achieve because we can be bombarded with professional learning and the last thing we want is for staff to get tired, and they are working really hard, and to be involved in professional learning that is not relevant to them. It starts from our strategic plan ... to make sure we are specific in our goals and clear about what we want to achieve to make sure that professional learning is streamlined toward meeting goals as whole staff.
>
> *(Male, government, primary, metropolitan, VIC)*

> The nature of quality professional learning, is that it is evidence based, problem based, as in problem solving, that it is based in the workplace and provides an opportunity for people to have expert external input, but internal application and feedback; that it is ongoing, systematic, individual, team and whole school.
>
> *(Male, government, secondary, metropolitan, NSW)*

This approach to professional learning has signalled a shift from the 'one-size', centralised workshops over the years to more school-based, initiated professional learning that better balances external and internal priorities.

> There was a time when the department would have said that professional learning was their responsibility, 'We will tell you what to do.' Through an industrial shift, we have had requirements for schools to engage in structured professional learning within their schools and show evidence of that, and be compliant and accountable around that. There would have been tension around that when it was introduced some years back, but now it is core business and we keep leveraging that because we know that through that we can get better outcomes in our classrooms, and stronger and more capable teachers.
>
> *(Male, government, secondary, metropolitan, ACT)*

> I think that professional learning is something we spend a lot of money on. I have concerns around the models of professional learning that see teachers go to conferences and workshops, externally provided sessions, without an implementation plan as to how that is going to help their practice in the classroom. Professional learning needs to be informing some change or some improvement or adjustment to teaching practice for it to be worthwhile rather than say I didn't get anything out of it to support my practice.
>
> *(Male, government, primary, metropolitan, ACT)*

Barriers to professional learning

While professional learning was almost universally recognised as key to school improvement, some mentioned cost as being a barrier, while a few principals of remote schools commented on the difficulty in having access to quality external professional learning.

> Face to face is difficult because of the distance. We provide money, release time, and support for people who want to increase their professional knowledge and skills. We had an EBA (enterprise bargaining agreement) meeting earlier this year and the teachers put forward that they wanted release time and money to support their learning, but there was no mention of Aboriginal support staff.
>
> *(Male, independent, secondary, very remote, NT)*

> Barriers can be money for the good stuff ... access [is a problem] in the Northern Territory. Access is a big issue to quality PD, and that involves getting people out because it's not necessarily available in the Northern Territory, and then getting permission for people to go out, that's a barrier.
>
> *(Female, government, preschool and primary, metropolitan, NT)*

Other means of developing staff and teams

Alongside setting up processes and structures, and providing time and the funding for developing themselves and others, principals spoke of many strategies they use to develop staff. Some of these include coaching, role review and clarity, use of professional standards and leadership profiles, sharing learning with others, distributive leadership, and building teams and capacity in others to support professional learning.

> We've engaged two full-time instructional coaches in leadership roles in our school. Their job is to work with teachers 100 per cent of the time to build their capacity, delivering professional learning, personalised if required. Working shoulder to shoulder, working on planning and assessment, videoing lessons – they could be modelling. People enrol [in coaching] based on their needs; it is not about addressing underperformance; it is a strength-based approach to help them improve.
>
> *(Male, government, primary, metropolitan, ACT)*

> You need to have pretty clear role descriptions for people so they are not guessing as to what it is you want them to do. Then, providing good skill training. We bring people in and we use our own expertise to skill people in running planning and reflective conversations. We offer targeted professional learning for leaders and aspiring leaders.
> *(Female, government, secondary, provincial, TAS)*

> The [Australian Professional] Standards, a picture of what constitutes quality, is essential within that. Once that is there, and people have an understanding of what that looks like, it becomes easier to establish goals and developmental processes along the way.
> *(Male, government, secondary, metropolitan, NSW)*

> I use the [AITSL] leadership profiles to develop my own leadership team. Four of my leadership team have undergone leadership accreditation this year, as I believe everybody needs to have the expertise and credibility for their leadership development. For heads of faculty to be credible to their teachers, they need to be at the top of their game.
> *(Female, government, P–10, metropolitan, ACT)*

> I'm building the capacity of others to lead not only their project, but to bring their team along, and this has been a very valuable initiative at our school, where folk have felt empowered in knowing what it entails to bring people along.
> *(Female, government, primary, metropolitan, QLD)*

Performance management: judgement and development

Twenty-two principals spoke of performance management as having two aspects: assessing performance, largely summative, and in the formative development of others.

> If you are going to have a culture of feedback, it cannot have even a touch of summative assessment. You have to keep the formative separate from the summative. If you are in the performance management mode, you make it explicit that it is summative, and concrete and hard edged, 'Yes, that's good enough', 'No, that's not.' It is very transactional. It needs to be clear cut as it may need to stand up in a HR sense, or industrial or court of law.
> *(Male, independent, P–12, metropolitan, VIC)*

> There has to be an accountability. People are trusting us with their children and that is a really important job. If someone is not giving of their best, then that shows pretty quickly. Schools are very public places. So, I begin with a conversation with a teacher around the craft of teaching, and if you don't see an improvement after that sort of intervention, then it becomes more targeted, taking minutes of the detail of what it is that someone needs to work on. I do see performance management as separate to performance development because I think if you try and bring the two together, the person is going to be worried about the management and not concentrating enough on the development. I think you need to be clear that they are two separate processes.
>
> *(Female, government, secondary girls, metropolitan, VIC)*

Not a 'quick-fix' solution

Professional learning policies and practices were seen as crucial, but not a 'quick-fix' simple solution, but more of an ongoing process.

> I think it's become ... seen by bureaucrats and politicians as the sort of quick-fix solution that all we have to do is make people do a certain amount of hours of professional learning a year, and then they'll be great teachers and all our problems will be over. But the quality of the professional learning is ... often so inferior that it's a waste of time.
>
> *(Male, independent, P–12, provincial, VIC)*

Wellbeing of self and others

Questions 11 and 12 asked principals to assess and comment on their current state of wellbeing, given their role, and to assess and comment on the current state of personal wellbeing of their staff. These questions also asked principals to comment on any strategies they employed to address wellbeing.

Personal wellbeing

Twenty-three principals – almost half – commented positively about their wellbeing; of these, 5 principals commented on having a strong sense of wellbeing, and being 'happy' and 'mentally strong' most of the time, while 18 of these principals commented more about being 'generally okay', 'reasonable', and 'pretty good'. Some acknowledged that wellbeing fluctuated depending on circumstances.

> My current state of wellbeing is reasonably good; ask me that a couple of weeks ago, it wasn't too good; at the beginning of the year it was absolutely shocking.
> *(Male, independent, P–12, metropolitan, QLD)*

> Very happy and very content, I am a high-energy person, and touch wood, healthy physically.
> *(Male, government, secondary, metropolitan, NSW)*

> I just completed the 2016 principal wellbeing survey and I am ok. I do this regularly and was able to track three recent years to see how I was going, even to the point of alcohol consumption, and the rating is okay.
> *(Male, government, secondary, metropolitan, ACT)*

Some attributed good wellbeing to general disposition (n=5), having a positive outlook (n=3) and a sense of humour (n=4).

> I don't stress, or get angry or raise my voice. It is about individual temperament. I see it as part of the job and there is no point of killing myself over something that is going on.
> *(Male, government, secondary 7–10, metropolitan, ACT)*

> I have a pretty good sense of humour, one of the things I have learned over a long period of time is to work out what are the things you are going to die on the hill over and be able to park some other things to the side if you need to, and don't overthink things.
> *(Male, government, secondary, metropolitan, VIC)*

> Obviously [as a new principal], I am still learning about this! I think you have to have a good sense of humour and put it into perspective.
> *(Female, Catholic, primary, metropolitan, SA)*

Strategies to maintain wellbeing

Principals mentioned various strategies to 'switch off', including putting their wellbeing 'first', knowing the signs when they are feeling stressed or need a break, trying to maintain a work–life balance, and the importance of leading by example in the area of wellbeing.

> I think as I've become a more experienced principal, I've learnt that it doesn't particularly make things any better or more productive if I spend long hours at work. I think maturity plays a part. I've learnt that there are other things in life that are just as important. I'm much more aware of not taking work home with me if I can help it.
>
> *(Female, government, early childhood–8, metropolitan, ACT)*

> I focus on not taking work home, and last weekend I decided to take my work emails off my phone and iPad. It was the result of some difficult conversations where some parents felt they had access to me 24/7 to discuss school issues. It has changed things a lot already. We have a home life that is separate to work.
>
> *(Male, government, primary, metropolitan, VIC)*

> I take one day a week off and clock out, I don't have difficulty do[ing] that anymore. I look after my mental and emotional health and wellbeing reasonably well.
>
> *(Male, independent, P–12, metropolitan, VIC)*

> I make sure I eat well, I don't exercise enough, I should, but I walk every day with my wife; that is really good.
>
> *(Male, independent, P–12, metropolitan, QLD)*

> On my way to school I stop at the gym for half an hour then shower and head off to work.
>
> *(Male, government, secondary, provincial, NSW)*

Knowing the signs

> You find out when you are stressed – when something goes wrong and you react to it. I know how I am faring because I respond well to situations and work through them successively.
>
> *(Female, government, P–12, very remote, WA)*

> I know when things get on top of me, my desk gets messy, I am not methodical, knowing the signs is important.
>
> *(Male, government, primary, metropolitan, VIC)*

Trying to maintain a work–life balance

> I guess my other part of my wellbeing is that having a balance in my life, and family, obviously, for me that's really important … I guess I believe that as a high-performing principal that your life is really integrated; it has to be. You can't kind of say, well, you know, this is my family life and this is my school life, you integrate it, but just making sure that within that integration that there's a balance, and that you're giving enough attention to the things and the people in your life that you care about.
>
> *(Female, government, preschool and primary, metropolitan, NT)*

> My job is my job, my profession is my profession, and my personal life is private. I find it difficult to have an outside hobby. I do leave work early one day a week. I try and model being pro-family. Family must come first, teaching is a profession and a job, but I tell my staff your family is more important. When the chips are down and deadlines need to be met, they are met, and then I tell my staff to go home.
>
> *(Female, government, P–10, metropolitan, ACT)*

> Try to stay fit, minimum amount of exercise every day, good relationship with my husband. We spend quality time together, play golf, switch off on holidays, sleep well at night. It is about work–life balance; you might be stressed if you didn't have a real connection with yourself … operating out of that deep knowledge.
>
> *(Female, Catholic, secondary, metropolitan, QLD)*

Leading by example

> I don't need to be the first person in the car park every morning and last every night. I encourage people to not spend all their time in there working. I have two children and I don't want to be the absent father. I have conversations with people about what is important. It is a narrative and a mindset, but it is leading by example.
>
> *(Male, government, primary, metropolitan, ACT)*

Support from others

Twenty-two principals spoke of the importance of having support from family, a partner, or colleagues in helping manage their wellbeing.

> [I] trust my senior management team, [we] share ... concerns or worries ... they can often be part of the solution. Keep a perspective because often the problem you think is the problem is not all that important if you consider other things that could be happening.
> *(Male, independent, P–12, metropolitan, VIC)*

> I ring a couple of mates. If I felt I was not able to manage the difficult things at work, I would go to a psychologist and have a conversation with them around some strategies.
> *(Female, government, secondary, provincial, TAS)*

> You know I get huge support ... I don't know if we're unique or not, but I have fantastic principal colleagues, and we spend a lot of time together, we have a lot of support meetings where, instead of everybody trying to take on everything individually, we kind of share the love, so that we're all working together to make sure that we get the tasks done, but kind of as smart as possible, rather than us all doing the same thing.
> *(Female, government, primary, metropolitan, NSW)*

> Yeah, I've got a couple of confidantes, which is lucky because without them I'd be really doing it hard I think. My wife is the main one, I must say.
> *(Male, independent, P–12, provincial, VIC)*

> I have an amazing husband, so I can debrief at home if I need to. He looks after me.
> *(Female, government, secondary, metropolitan, QLD)*

Workload and stress

While 23 principals spoke of positive aspects to wellbeing, nearly half of the principals – an equal number – mentioned feelings of stress (n=23) and the effects the role had on their wellbeing.

> I am extremely happy in my role. I love being a principal. It is a privilege to be a principal, but there is a price. And that price is to do with family, and health. I don't exercise as much as I should. I eat really well. I am extremely lucky;

in a position where I have the total support of my family in the role that I am in. They realise there are nights when I won't be home until after 10pm, or nights when I can't leave school between after-school meetings and evening commitments, or that I will be called back on weekends.
(Female, government, primary, metropolitan, VIC)

At risk. I mean that not in a dangerous way, the role is very demanding and consuming, and impacts on the amount of sleep I get, the time I have to spend with my family, how much downtime I get, it is not just the hours, it is the emotional drain as well. Every time there is a situation that involves people that has not had an ideal outcome, it is all those things that sit in the back of my mind.
(Female, government, primary, remote, WA)

This is an area that I have struggled with for the last 30 years. I do have a tendency to put the needs of others ahead of myself, both as a person and a principal. I do have a tendency to look at how I could have done things differently to make things happen a different way. There have been a few times in my career where I have taken time out for depression, I am open about it and tell people that I have depression and I am taking medication. Right now, I am about 50/50.
(Female, government, primary, metropolitan, WA)

We have been doing a lot of work in the principal leadership team in my network. We had a significant number of leaders going off on stress or having heart attacks. I have a belief in why it happens, partly [the lack of] system support, partly the impact parents have at school and how we best manage them.
(Male, Catholic, primary, provincial, VIC)

Role conflict and complexity

The complexity of the role (n=15) and long work hours (n=16) was attributed to some principals' sense of poor wellbeing. Five principals mentioned compliance demands, while another 5 spoke of the lack of support from others as contributing to their negative sense of wellbeing.

Keep politicians out of it. Give a bit more professional integrity to the principals. Don't dump stuff on [every principal] when five or ten people in

CHAPTER 7: Developing self and others

> the bureaucracy steal money or behave dishonourably – don't make every school in Victoria pay for it.
>
> *(Male, government, primary, metropolitan, VIC)*

> The compliance in the ACT is becoming phenomenal. It is for the sake of compliance. The ACT is so small and everyone has direct access to the government. A lot of it is keeping schools out of the newspaper. The paperwork that is coming from our directorate, everyone says that schools are much more autonomous, but they are not because the directorate is unwilling/will not go down the independent public route because they are too small, so principals here will never be autonomous. We will never be able to work with school boards. I would say morale amongst ACT principals has dropped hugely and now we are all legally responsible personally. Even when I am off sick and something goes wrong here, I am still legally responsible. I had a major operation, but still had to check in daily, still had to answer emails, had to jump through emails for the directorate.
>
> *(Female, government, P–10, metropolitan, ACT)*

> Yeah, the amount of paperwork and red tape has increased since I started 11 years ago. I'd say it's increased 60 per cent maybe.
>
> *(Male, independent, P–12, provincial, VIC)*

> As a principal, I feel we are out there working in silos. The department will pull the mat out from underneath you if you make a mistake. They are not supporting young principals really well. It is easy to make a mistake, it is easy to overlook something or miss something, and that support is not there.
>
> *(Female, government, primary, metropolitan, VIC)*

Attending to staff wellbeing

The state of staff wellbeing

Twenty-one principals – a minority – reported the general wellbeing of their staff as being 'good' and 'generally okay', while some (n=7) spoke of staff wellbeing being cyclical, 'dependent on the time of year'.

> [This is] one of the things that we have done really well in ... overall, the staff wellbeing is strong, we have very small staff turnover, people are happy and

> not looking to move, and [there are] plenty who want to come, to apply for positions, but we don't actually have any.
>
> *(Male, government, primary, metropolitan, ACT)*

> You have to be working in a school to understand the pressures of a term, reporting and parents, it is a crescendo and you are pushed through an hour glass. I hope staff can then find ways to experience relaxation.
>
> *(Male, independent, P–12, metropolitan, NSW)*

> End of term, pretty bad. Staff anywhere will work hard. I do make them work hard to be honest as I have high expectations of them. But I would also argue that if someone is not working hard, then their heart is not in the job.
>
> *(Male, independent, P–12, metropolitan, QLD)*

Strategies addressing staff wellbeing

Principals spoke of a range of strategies when it came to addressing and managing staff wellbeing. Some of these included creating a staff wellbeing role, acknowledging staff accomplishment, providing professional learning, having flexibility and supporting staff needs, and providing a range of social events and activities.

> Well one of my APs is [supporting staff] ... we've got a staff coach and her role is to work with staff in relation to their own professional growth, but we've also [got] a person from the teachers' side who's a wellbeing person, and we also have one of our office staff ... office manager and ... people will go and talk to her.
>
> *(Male, government, primary, metropolitan, VIC)*

> I think we are open and accommodating for personal leave. If someone needs to attend a funeral I would never hesitate, if they are going to be late in or have an appointment, we try to accommodate that, as long as it is not on a regular basis, they know there is give and take.
>
> *(Male, government, primary, metropolitan, VIC)*

> We have an after-school fitness class, [and a] staff health and wellbeing bulletin that goes out every Friday afternoon with a couple of simple recipes for the weekend.
>
> *(Male, government, secondary, metropolitan, NSW)*

> Wellbeing committee, we use Mindmatters, humour, prayer, laughter, celebrations. Staff are resilient. Making personal time with people, quiet behind the scenes and affirming good practice in public forums. Also, not shoving under the carpet the things that are not working well. It is like a see-saw, everything that is going well opens another opportunity for us to work on other stuff. Understanding differentiation and the needs of individual learners, and reminding them that structures need to reflect our core principles rather than drive them.
> *(Female, Catholic, P–12, provincial, SA)*

The importance of school culture to staff wellbeing

Many principals commented on the importance of culture, and of putting in place strategies and processes to support staff wellbeing.

> So, the number one thing is ... [about wellbeing] I work on the school culture first.
> *(Female, government, primary, metropolitan, VIC)*

> We grapple with many issues on a human level before you even get to the teaching and learning, and [the] strategic plan and pushing ahead with NAPLAN results, and so on. And those issues are so important – that I [need to] get the management and the support right – it is 'the way we do things around here'. We support one another, and we make sure that everyone is well and is coping with some of the issues they have inside and outside the school, and that is one of the strengths of the culture of my school.
> *(Female, government, primary, metropolitan, VIC)*

> We provide them with space. It is the strong collaborative team culture and systems in place to support them and acknowledge that they are busy.
> *(Female, government, secondary, provincial, TAS)*

> It is highly collegial, there is a clear sense of purpose and direction. There is a real commitment by almost everyone to an inclusive and welcoming nature. Pride and accomplishment of our achievements, which are manifold. We are in a very good place.
> *(Male, Catholic, secondary, metropolitan, ACT)*

Conclusion

There was general agreement of the desirable qualities and actions for being a 'good' principal. These traits and behaviours were somewhat visionary and altruistic, yet realistic for what the role entails. What came through strongly was recognition of the importance of personal values, high expectations of self and others, role modelling, respect, drive, and vision for what principals are trying to achieve in their school, as well as the necessity of being able to work through and with others to achieve this.

Knowing staff as people, learners and educators, and building and maintaining appropriate relationships were also key. Once again there was strong support for and commitment to professional learning, both for staff and others, in changing and improving the school.

The importance of personal wellbeing and the wellbeing of staff was recognised, as were the work pressures that tend to undermine mental health. A worrying proportion of principals – around half – shared concerns about their wellbeing, while detailing means in which they attempted to cope with the pressures of the job. Support from others, colleagues and family members, was seen as vital in this regard. Similarly, around half of those interviewed expressed concern for the wellbeing of their staff and, once again, there were various ways that principals attempted to 'look after' them.

Finally, there was general concern with the mounting externally imposed mandatory administrative and compliance requirements on schools in all sectors. Principals saw this as not facilitating their core business of leading learning and teaching, but of impacting negatively upon them and those with whom they work.

CHAPTER 8
Leading improvement, innovation and change

Introduction
At this point in the interview schedule (see Appendix) there were four questions devoted to exploring 'Leading Improvement, Innovation and Change', one of five aspects of the 'Professional Practices' outlined in the Australian Professional Standard for Principals.

These questions, numbered 14–17, enabled principals to reflect on their leadership of improvement, innovation and change in terms of what they were doing and had accomplished, and what they hoped or intended to achieve over time. The questions were broad in nature, and principals offered insight into their own learning as well as the processes of change and improvement they are leading within their school. It is acknowledged that some comments relevant to this area have arisen in other chapters due to inevitable overlap, but each adds to the overall picture of the work of the principal. The purpose of these questions were to ask the principals to:

14. describe their vision for their school and what they are trying to achieve
15. outline what the three most important issues to be addressed at their school in the next five years were
16. list the strategies they employ to implement, monitor and measure the impact of school plans and policies
17. add anything else they would like about leading improvement, innovation and change.

Setting a vision for the school

When asked Question 14, 'What is your vision for your school? What are you trying to achieve?', all principals were quick to respond, indicating that this vision was both clear in their minds and significant. The principals were able to clearly articulate what many described as a 'pathway', a 'journey', a course of action or a staged approach to a preferred future for their school.

Assisting students to be active, effective, global citizens

While there were a variety of responses to the question on vision, the most common that emerged was that principals were seeking to create a school culture, or learning environment, that had a focus on universal or international perspectives. This was to prepare their students for life in a changing world, not just academic success.

> [To put an] emphasis on internationalising our education program because it is really important that we recognise that we are just a part of the whole world, not just on our own out here.
> *(Male, government, primary, metropolitan, VIC)*

There were 18 principals who offered reflections in this regard, such as a desire for a connectedness between the school and broader society, and recognition of the need to prepare young people locally for a future that was globally relevant. A further aspect of this was on working with students to understand their place in the community.

> For me it is bigger than just NAPLAN or Year 12 results or getting kids into university; it is far bigger than that. It is actually about preparing and equipping young people to make a positive difference, and be successful in the communities in which they will live and work when they leave school.
> *(Male, independent, P–12, metropolitan, QLD)*

> We are trying to give the kids the skills to be active citizens in the future, but it is not about the individual, they need to understand that they are part of a community, and they have a responsibility to that community as well as the global community, actively engaged with what is going on in the world. Educating for today and tomorrow.
> *(Female, government, secondary, provincial, TAS)*

> My vision is to drag the school into the international sphere because 150 years ago there was Anangu [Indigenous people] separate from white fellas, now it is like Anangu is in the middle, like a little circle inside a big white Australia. That has been the situation here for the last 50 years, but now, in education, we are part of the world. It is important for our kids and people to see what people do in other states and communities, and what is happening in the world. I am keen to push that agenda ... for our kids to be confident global citizens, our kids eat witchetty grubs and they also like iPhone 6. They hunt goannas, but they love watching YouTube ... they have to be confident and competent in the two ways.
>
> *(Male, independent, secondary, very remote, NT)*

Developing the whole child for the future

Six principals spoke about developing the whole child, a focus on character, developing intellectual and emotional intelligence, and building on the strengths of the individual.

> I am creating an environment that is creating future citizens, so we can't focus on one area of a successful person. I am less about the academic and more about the whole child. I want everyone to focus on it.
>
> *(Female, government, primary, metropolitan, WA)*

> What we are trying to achieve is children who develop as whole people, for our kids, in our context, it is about a sense of self, connection to country and community. Valuing their Aboriginal identity in who they are. Our vision is students are empowered and engaged learners, caring for their community and their country. They are strong in their culture and have strong academic skills to be actively informed community members, who positively contribute to life across the [community].
>
> *(Female, government, P–12, very remote, WA)*

> I want to help students become effective adults, and by effective I mean people who can think creatively and imaginatively and flexibly. People who can engage in good relationships in the workplace and in their personal lives. People who can feel a sense of satisfaction with their achievements, and who can experience a full range of emotions, and I also want them to grow intellectually as well as academically.
>
> *(Male, independent, P–12, provincial, VIC)*

Doing what's best for the child
Seven principals focused their school vision on providing what is best for the child – what could be described as a learner- or student-centred culture.

> I think that the bottom line has to … always be what's best for the kids, and we put a lot of work into that.
> *(Male, government, primary, metropolitan, VIC)*

> Doing the best we can for all of our children, which is a very obvious answer, but our vision statement is 'Together we create the future', and that is the way we do our stuff at our school. So, it's doing the very best we possibly can each day, and together we will do that, we will create that future.
> *(Female, government, primary, metropolitan, QLD)*

> I want every young person to be able to solve problems, work in teams, manage complexity and change, and always have a joyful hope about what they are, who they are and how they connect to the world.
> *(Female, Catholic, P–12, provincial, SA)*

A professional learning community characterised by innovation
The importance and role of professional learning in improving teaching and learning has been highlighted in other chapters. Principals commented on seeking to create a professional learning community within their schools, and that this was a core component of their vision for the school. Their comments reflected the need for all members of the community to identify as learners, including parents, staff and students. There was also a common reference to responsibility and accountability, meaning that in a high-performing community of learners, all members accept responsibility for the culture and the learning environment.

> [My vision is] … having a really high-functioning professional learning community where teachers are working collaboratively and they take a collaborative responsibility or a joint responsibility for every child, not just the ones who are on their class roll.
> *(Female, government, secondary, metropolitan, ACT)*

Four principals extended their comments to include ways in which a professional learning community establishes its own culture of innovation.

> I'd like the school to have mechanisms to generate ideas and promote them – to land them, to implement them. I'd like staff to have a forum to be able to put ideas forward that might be considered or might make us do things better – be courageous in their innovation.
>
> *(Male, Catholic, secondary, metropolitan, ACT)*

> The management or ethos of the school is to say it is all right to give things a go. Let's be innovative; let's take a few risks and not stay in that safe zone all the time otherwise we become custodians and we don't move forward. My key message there is that you cannot rely on the vision just being articulated by the principal; it needs to come from different voices at different times and in different environments.
>
> *(Male, government, primary, metropolitan, VIC)*

Big issues to be addressed in the next five years

Question 15 invited principals to reflect on what they see as the three most important issues or main areas for change or improvement for their school in the next five years. The following themes or issues emerged: staffing for quality teaching, staff professional development, improving the quality of teaching and pedagogy, sustaining growth (enrolments, building programs and resourcing), technology, mental health and wellbeing, developing leadership in others, building community partnerships and parental engagement, raising aspirations and the use of data.

Staffing for quality teaching

A slight majority of principals (n=26) nominated staffing and improving the quality of teaching as key areas of focus in the next five years. Reflecting earlier comments, principals noted that investing in the 'right' teachers was paramount.

> Staffing, getting the best teachers. It is often underestimated how important that is. I don't have contract staff. I advertise for ongoing staff, so they know they don't have to worry about end of contract, etc. We do mock interviews

[to prepare teacher candidates] ... we have a lot of fourth year [BEd] students coming through, so we have the opportunity to get the best graduates through that process. We have a lot of great mentor teachers who will work well with them. I keep the interview process open for three or four weeks – get the word out and let as many people know as possible; encourage them to come and visit, have a school tour.

(Male, government, primary, metropolitan, VIC)

I am grappling with staffing at the moment. It is causing me great angst. We have sufficient applicants, but it is getting the right people with the right skills. A love of children and those with children at the centre of their decision making. Someone who doesn't fit in with a child-centred culture will really stand out. I'm finding a lot of young people have anxiety, they are away a lot. It is impacting on the staffing at present.

(Female, government, primary, metropolitan, VIC)

Under the enterprise agreement teachers have to move every five years, so maintaining a balanced profile from a school autonomy perspective and maintaining pay scales is going to be extremely difficult. People want to get rid of their expensive teachers and employ the cheaper alternative. The IB [International Baccalaureate] is quite specialised with expensive professional development that focuses on maintaining the international feel of the school.

(Female, government, P–12, metropolitan, ACT)

I would love to be able to see teachers stay in remote locations longer that the standard two years. We get young people who haven't been able to get jobs elsewhere. We get people who have sent their kids off to uni or work or people who have finished their football career. So, the sort of people we get tend to be quite different. They tend to be adventurous which means they tend to move on to other adventures ... If there was some way of attracting people to come and stay for a longer time it would be good.

(Male, independent, secondary, very remote, NT)

Staff professional development

As highlighted in previous responses, principals are seeking to create a school culture where all participants recognise themselves as learners and exhibit a willingness to grow and improve. Investment in quality professional learning for staff was offered by principals (n=17) as a key area for focus in the next five years, and included developing teacher-to-teacher and teacher-to-student feedback processes with a focus on pedagogy and teacher collaboration.

> Good outcomes for kids depends on having great teachers, so continually finding ways to build the capacity of the workforce; that is, teaching and non-teaching staff to support outcomes for kids [is a priority].
> *(Male, government, secondary, metropolitan, VIC)*

> ... school staff engaged with research is one thing, and I don't mean just reading it, I mean actually engaging with it ... to try and implement more practically the school vision.
> *(Female, government, primary, provincial, NSW)*

> To know the current research around early practice ... we know so much more now about brain development and child development that's come out ... even in the last five years, we know so much more about that, and that informs our practice and ... that information often changes our practice. So, in the next five years, I think it's important that we continue to study the current research and to use that research to inform our practice.
> *(Female, government, primary, metropolitan, ACT)*

> Building teacher capacities and getting our teachers to the point where they are self-motivated around their learning, that they understand where they're at, and that they're actively advancing their own learning and working in their teams to continue the learning of the team that's really site-based learning, hands-on learning, and so there's certainly elements of that, and some teams are working really well, so that will definitely continue.
> *(Female, government, primary, metropolitan, NT)*

Improving the quality of teaching and pedagogy

Continuing on for the theme of teacher professional learning is the perceived outcome of such an investment, that is, continuous improvement in pedagogy and the quality of teaching. There were 18 principals who identified improving pedagogy and the quality of teaching as a major issue over the coming five years:

> Improving the quality of teaching in the delivery of learning. It is a structured plan; the executive is involved, and it is about looking at learning goals and

> high expectations, and high-quality work. I am going on class next year myself and modelling it.
>
> *(Male, government, secondary, provincial, NSW)*

> Quality teaching – strengthen quality professional learning and practice.
>
> *(Male, Catholic, primary, provincial, VIC)*

> The most attractive thing for us is the quality of our teaching and learning, improving pedagogy in whatever areas possible. The driving force behind all of this comes from the McKinsey report, a focus on teachers, focus on retaining quality, quality teaching practice, and a big area would be high expectations, what you can do to improve expectations of self and others.
>
> *(Male, independent, P–12, metropolitan, VIC)*

There were specific aspects of teaching or pedagogy noted by principals in these responses. These included a focus on differentiation or personalisation of student learning, the provision of effective feedback to students, improving literacy and numeracy, and the design and implementation of new curriculum and school structures that enable creative or innovative approaches to catering for the diverse needs of students.

> We have been working on pedagogy and differentiation for the last couple of years, we are wanting to get closer to personalised learning – getting better at it. I want to break out of it a little bit, out of the traditional grouping that we have. Even though we have the Australian Curriculum, that keeps us in little boxes. How we can break out of that to a degree and have a lot more cross-age learning that is relevant to particular children, so that the learning is personalised and how we can go about organising our school around it.
>
> *(Female, Catholic, primary, metropolitan, SA)*

> …our priorities, literacy, numeracy and pedagogical practice. We have other things as well that support that, for example, student outcomes across the board. We have a whole new system coming in for senior students, new syllabuses aligned with ACARA, but kids aren't going to achieve there if they don't have literacy and numeracy under their belt. If teachers don't have the skills that they need to be able to challenge the students, differentiate for our students, or select pedagogical practices to match the needs of our students, then they will not get the literacy, numeracy outcomes either.
>
> *(Female, government, secondary, metropolitan, QLD)*

> Literacy outcomes for our students. We are continuously working in this space and we are in an upward trend but we are not value adding to the extent that I would like. Our focus must remain on literacy, as it sits at the basis of everything for all of our kids.
>
> *(Female, government, secondary, provincial, TAS)*

> One of the most exciting things we are doing next year is moving to a vertical tutor system where students are in vertical tutor groups rather than horizontal tutor groups, and that is the stepping stone to vertical learning. Within the next five years, we will challenge the whole notion of grade levels and why we are teaching kids in grade levels ... vertical learning rather than just learning that is based on their age. That is going to be a really exciting thing that we are looking at and challenging.
>
> *(Male, independent, P–12, metropolitan, QLD)*

Sustaining growth – enrolments, building programs, resourcing

There were 15 principals who indicated that sustainability or growth in some form or other was a priority in the coming five years. For some principals this meant obtaining or maintaining the resources required to cater for their students, for others it signified a focus on enrolments, building programs or balancing finances.

> My main issue is not a curriculum issue, it is working with the bureaucracy to sustain the school growth, and control the growth, and provide the facilities that are necessary to cope with that growth.
>
> *(Male, government, primary, metropolitan, VIC)*

> Being able to provide sufficient resources to create learning environments that allow kids to experience the learning growth that they need, so developing a physical and virtual learning environment, trying to do more with less, or trying to do more with just the resources you have now. So, finding other partners who can help with the work, community-based or industry-based partners, other schools, building networks to assist in that process is going to be critical.
>
> *(Male, government, secondary, metropolitan, VIC)*

> Upgrading buildings. We look to double in size between now and 2020 due to new land released by the government. That is going to be an enormous project management initiative with the increased student population and building size. The repercussions will be maintaining the school culture, maintaining the IB profile and ensuring the school does not change as a result of the increased enrolment.
> *(Female, government, P–12, metropolitan, ACT)*

> We are already over capacity. We are heading toward 1300 or more [students], so managing the growth. The numbers start to change the way the school actually works.
> *(Male, government, secondary, metropolitan, VIC)*

> How we genuinely meet the needs of all of our students as we continue to grow at such a rate that may not be sustainable. What does it mean to be running a primary school with more than 1100 students? What are the risks that come with that? Does it mean we don't know them? And what are we going to put in place to ensure that never occurs? How do they feel relevant?
> *(Male, government, primary, metropolitan, VIC)*

> The demographic of the school continues to change with more English as Second Language students coming into the school. Because of where the school is situated, it's considered a prime area for settlement for refugee families, and families that come from war-torn countries and traumatic backgrounds. This school has a very solid reputation of supporting those families and those students, and building their capacity to adapt to their new country, and to learn English and work within our very English-based system.
> *(Female, government, primary, provincial, NSW)*

Technology

There were 17 principals who noted the provision of technology and its use as one of their big three issues into the future.

> ... moving forward with our technology and ICT, the whole STEM thing and how we are going to fit that in, and what that is going to mean for how we go forward with those things.
> *(Female, Catholic, primary, metropolitan, SA)*

[We are] in the process of introducing a BYOD [bring your own device] initiative. We are using Google Apps for education and trying to make it a paperless staffroom. Introducing BYOD is not a case of students bringing computers in, it is teaching teachers to improve or enhance the quality of the learning through digital technology.

(Female, government, P–12, metropolitan, ACT)

How we embed the digital technologies into the work in the school, particularly with the notion that NAPLAN is going online. Maximising our digital interface with the student's skills is a concern.

(Female, government, primary, metropolitan, WA)

Digital technology is one I am working closely on with my board. Being in a low-SES community, there is an equity issue around access to connectivity, for example. We have surveyed our parents and found out that many of them don't have access to the internet outside of the school, and don't have the finances to be doing BYOD or providing contributions for devices, so we have been looking at cost-effective ways of doing that. We have been looking at Google Chrome books that are inexpensive and efficient. We have provided one-to-one to our students from Years 3–6, so at least we know they have strong access to the digital world, at least while within the school environment.

(Male, government, primary, metropolitan, ACT)

The effective use of learning technologies is a really big and simple example – how do we ensure we don't have 'edutainment', but learning technologies that are about helping enrich the learning? Many teachers struggle with how [to] use it well, wisely – improving over old technologies of talking face to face, writing with pen and paper, etc.

(Male, government, secondary, metropolitan, ACT)

We need to get our kids more technologically advanced than what they are now. Our kids can use iPads to do basic stuff, but they don't use them in a way that assists or challenges their learning.

(Male, independent, secondary, very remote, NT)

Mental health and wellbeing

There were 9 principals who highlighted the management of mental health issues and awareness among students and staff as a significant area of concern over the next five years. Principals indicated that they had noticed a rise in the number of mental health issues in young people and the challenges that their school faces to adequately cater for the needs of young people in this area.

> Increased levels of anxiety and mental health issues in kids. How do we reduce these? How do we promote a positive growth mindset?
> *(Male, independent, P–12, metropolitan, NSW)*

> Relationships with our students, particularly due to our turnover. Our township ... provides government housing, [there's] not a lot of industry ... 60 per cent of our families are Indigenous families. The turnover is quite high because of the Indigeneity and the public housing. A child will enter and exit up to three times over the year so there is a lot of disruption to learning and no continuity. So that our kids feel safe [and] connect with people when they come here, we put a focus on the social [and] emotional wellbeing so that we can then get academic learning. Addressing the wellbeing of kids is pretty key at our school, and ensuring they have positive interactions with staff and each other.
> *(Female, government, P–12, remote, NT)*

> The identification, management and support of an increasing number of mental health issues for students, to a degree for staff, but mainly for students ... in the broader community the resourcing is just not there to provide the kind of support that students need increasingly in a highly stressed community.
> *(Male, government, secondary, metropolitan, NSW)*

> One of the priorities we have next year is to start with the staff and then move to the students – the notion of positive psychology and resilience. This is not a program; it is an approach that needs to be embedded in everyday life at the school. Young people seeing themselves in a positive light. That is not saying we don't raise areas that they need to continue to grow in, but we need to give them the skills, and it needs to be an approach, not a four-week program.
> *(Male, government, primary, metropolitan, VIC)*

Developing leadership in others

Eight principals recognised the need for leadership within the school and the system, and identified the development of leadership in others as an area of focus for the next five years. These principals saw it as part of their responsibility to provide leadership opportunities, foster leadership development in teachers and encourage the take-up of leadership roles.

> Making sure I have good people coming through and giv[ing] them every opportunity to develop them as leaders. The system needs people to be interested in leadership. I run an internal leadership program and anyone who is interested in leadership can come along. We meet twice a term and I share readings, articles, stories, TED Talks. I have 13 staff involved in this – more than half the staff – I'm really proud of that. It is something I am really trying to develop.
>
> *(Male, government, primary, metropolitan, VIC)*

> The development of an increased leadership density. We have had some extraordinary things occur in our school in the last few years. The outcome has been an extraordinarily high rate of promotion, so we have lost a lot of highly capable leaders. It is not as though we don't have them coming through, we do, but there is a gap at the moment. We have picked up a lot of young fantastic teachers.
>
> *(Male, government, secondary, metropolitan, NSW)*

> Building the right sort of leadership teams within the school and having a degree of agility with how the teams come together, form, do the work, potentially dissolve, and start on what is next. The notion of having permanent leadership teams that are always at the centre may need to change. We need a more agile approach to change.
>
> *(Male, government, secondary, metropolitan, VIC)*

> Developing young leaders ... throughout the school. A lot of people perhaps now have ... moved their way through the system and have become at the top of the classroom teacher range, and we're sort of short-circuiting that and we're trying to bring on young people ... to develop them first of all as year-level leaders, and then, as leading teachers at the school, to develop their abilities and to develop their interest in taking on leadership roles because

> it's really, really important to have teachers who want to take on that role [of] leading learning within the school.
>
> *(Male, government, primary, metropolitan, VIC)*

Building community partnerships and parental engagement

There were 12 principals who indicated they would concentrate on building community partnerships and parental engagement over the next five years. Some of the reasons they cited were to connect students more readily with the broader community, or to connect parents more deeply with the school and their child's learning.

> What we are doing is trying to build our partnerships with the business community; our senior students have a business community mentor, so we can link them with real-life experiences, contributing back into the community.
>
> *(Female, government, secondary, metropolitan, QLD)*

> I think working with our community better – the liaison with health at the system level and bringing it down to the local level – in a network of schools and in the health network, building the capacity within the hospital for our school to better meet the needs of students, but within the framework of a health setting, and communicating the changes with our partners; better networking and better communication.
>
> *(Female, government, hospital school, metropolitan, NSW)*

> One of the more successful strategies is inviting parents to the school for learning journeys so they can see inside classrooms and how things operate. We also use our social media platforms, using photographs and images and videos to give parents insights into classrooms – it has been successful in communicating with parents, not just for operational things, but to provide some clear messaging around why we are doing certain things in the classroom, what our response is to homework; it is helping to undo some of the entrenched models around what school looks like.
>
> *(Male, government, primary, metropolitan, ACT)*

Raising aspirations

Five principals referenced raising the aspirations of their students as one of their big three issues for the next five years – to challenge students to aim high, and set high expectations for their own learning and their future.

> It is important for us to be able lift the aspirations of our students. In our community there is a bit of a belief that you can't achieve really high ... we want kids to aspire and do well. We are finding that a number of our students struggle with complex higher-order skills, so teaching those is important.
> *(Female, government, secondary, metropolitan, QLD)*

> To reassure the community and the students and develop an understanding that they can do it. Mine is a low-SES community, so that whole notion about expectations and aspirations is a significant issue for us. Sometimes there is a defeatist mentality. We spend a lot of time on this; it is an ongoing challenge.
> *(Male, government, secondary, metropolitan, NSW)*

> The culture of learning ... is not at a level where it will be successful if it's not focused on a sense of low self-efficacy and a sense of apathy amongst many of the students. They don't believe that they can succeed, and we need to change that mindset, not just of the students, but many of the teachers have a fixed mindset around the capability of many of our students.
> *(Female, government, secondary, metropolitan, ACT)*

The use of data

Five principals commented on the collection, analysis and application of data to inform change and improvement as a priority area for the future. Some were focused on the use of data as evidence to shape curriculum planning and to develop consistent in-school processes for monitoring student learning and engagement; others reflected on the lack of transference of longitudinal student achievement data across state and territory boundaries, and the impact that this had on schools seeking to cater for transient students.

> The appropriate use of data, how staff seek out data, discuss it and implement changes in their practice in accordance with what that data says. We are getting better at measuring growth rather than absolute achievement – look

at where they started and finished. How you measure the non-cognitive skills; we, or the world, have not cracked that one yet.

(Male, independent, P–12, metropolitan, VIC)

Strategies used to implement, monitor and measure impact

Question 16 asked principals to reflect on the strategies they employ to implement, monitor and measure the impact of school plans and policies. Principals offered insight into a number of enabling strategies to successful implementation, monitoring, and measuring of school plans and policies.

> Clear communication, ensuring the goals are smart and realistic, measureable, goals that can apply to the whole school, ensuring if there is professional learning and development required that it is well resourced, bringing in academic experts to upskill the staff, encouraging a culture where it is okay to fail, you want people to keep taking risks and improving. By our nature, the beauty of positive education and positive learning, there is no limit on the enthusiasm of our staff, these things constantly change and evolve, there are always things people can do to get better.
>
> *(Male, independent, P–12, metropolitan, VIC)*

> … it is important to have consultative mechanisms in place where you involve all stakeholders – that will help in the implementation stage as everyone will own it, it will be ratified at school board level but before the ratification process, people have had plenty of time, everyone has had a chance to be involved.
>
> *(Female, Catholic, primary, metropolitan, SA)*

Strategic planning and plans

In terms of implementation of innovation, improvement and change, 13 principals referred to their school's strategic plan as a key resource and means for maintaining clear direction as well as monitoring progress. They also referred to additional plans or policies that interconnected with their strategic plan. These documents were variously referred to as action plans, school improvement plans, policy implementation plans, or annual operating plans.

CHAPTER 8: Leading improvement, innovation and change

> We have a five-year strategic plan, but also yearly school plans that have targets and measures built-in. That allows us in an ongoing way to consider our accountability for student achievement and build staff capacity.
> *(Male, government, primary, metropolitan, ACT)*

> We have four key drivers within our strategic plan, linked to our values and behavioural expectations that are in a neat diagram that everyone acts upon. There are KPIs for those goals.
> *(Female, government, secondary, provincial, TAS)*

> Our strategic plan is very new. I make sure everyone has a copy of our strategic plan and annual improvement plan, so they know what the school is working towards, and we link that in with their PDP so their professional goals have a direct line of sight back to our strategic plan. We use stoplights to monitor our goals: green, amber, red. We have only just presented it to the school council and you can see visually very clearly what we are going well on, what we have just started on, what we have not started. In six months, we have done really well.
> *(Female, government, primary, metropolitan, VIC)*

> Every leadership meeting ... the strategic plan and the annual operating plan are pulled out to make sure we don't stray too far from it.
> *(Male, Catholic, P–12, provincial, SA)*

> [The] '5P[s:]' ... processes, purpose, people, planning and product, we look at the people involved and regularly monitor what is going on. It is a shared development process that involves lots of community consultation.
> *(Male, government, secondary, provincial, NSW)*

Principals were able to identify how the strategic plan influenced the development of professional action plans or performance plans for staff.

> We build the performance and development plan for each individual teacher from the annual implementation plan. That has enough scope in there for diversity, but it means that [teachers can say,] 'I understand why I am doing this', because it is part of the bigger picture of this school. It is a cascading view from strategic plan to annual implementation plan to the professional development plan for individual staff members. Performance is built-in there.
> *(Male, government, primary, metropolitan, VIC)*

Principals indicated that the strategic plan also enabled them to identify where to apply focus and to not overcommit to multiple priorities or areas of need.

> We have a clear, but focused strategic plan. It is short and to the point. We work on a few things and do them well. That flows on to the others.
> *(Male, independent, P–12, metropolitan, SA)*

Monitoring progress

Principals identified multiple strategies for monitoring progress of school plans and policies. Their comments reflected an action orientation where the concept of monitoring or evaluation was integrated into regular practice.

> In terms of monitoring, making sure you have a system in place, a clear review date when things are ratified and [that] those things happen on that date. Generally, it is every couple of years for policies, for processes. I think people need to be able to have input about how things work. That is why you have communication mechanisms. I am always open to hearing from people about how things could operate more smoothly, and I am always open to changing them. That is a good thing about being in a small school; it is easy because you don't have to consult with so many people.
> *(Female, Catholic, primary, metropolitan, SA)*

> The team meets regularly to actually unpack the area that they're responsible for tracking, so they're constantly looking for evidence that we are meeting our targets, or that we're moving towards them.
> *(Male, Catholic, secondary, metropolitan, VIC)*

Teachers as enablers and contributors

Eleven principals made specific reference to teachers as key contributors or enablers when it comes to the implementation of school plans. This related to the impact that teachers have in the classroom, the connection that teachers make to the strategic plan through their professional learning plans, and the interactions between staff to ensure a collaborative approach to achieving the school's intent.

> I have a very, very effective team of teachers. In fact I'd be hard pressed to think of another school where there are better teachers. They are really absolutely fantastic and I've given them the freedom to not only write the challenges that we [identify] ... obviously, I've got to approve them, but they write what they think are the challenges coming up, and we don't set easy ones, and because they've got skin in the game, it's been quite easy to ensure that those challenges are all met. So, we set very ambitious performance targets, and we have some outstanding student achievement ... for me it's quite easy to lead a school where the teachers are actually pushing the improvements themselves supported by the administration.
>
> *(Male, government, primary, metropolitan, VIC)*

> Involving teachers ... in the decision-making process, they're usually very quick to tell you what they believe is going to work or not work, or if things need refining. For example, I've got a group of Year 6 teachers who are observing the Year 4 teachers' writing lessons because there are certain things about the pedagogy of writing that we're implementing in our school that we know our Year 6 teachers could benefit from.
>
> *(Female, government, primary, metropolitan, QLD)*

> Teachers ... reference the strategic work of the school in their own performance and development plans. The conversations ... happen in smaller groups with other colleagues and the leader of the team. Having it up front and centre in the work you do in the school is really important.
>
> *(Male, government, secondary, metropolitan, VIC)*

School culture and collaboration

References were made by 4 principals to 'school culture' and 'a readiness for collaboration for learning' as being contributing factors in the implementation phase of a school plan or initiative.

> Not only have [teachers] opened the [classroom] doors, but people are seeking opportunities to go and watch others, and work out how they can improve their strategies in their own environment. So, having staff that take the initiative and use innovation has been huge, and I guess they're able to identify teacher experts in different areas and go to those people. So, the collegiality around that has really improved, and I feel like we're on a bit of a wave at the moment. Improvement is not necessarily pushed by me; it's become a collaborative staff culture where everybody knows that's the goal, and it really isn't led by

> me. I guess it still is led by me, but before it was ... very much me on my own pushing that kind of bandwagon, but now everyone's onboard ... the collaboration around innovation and change is really huge.
>
> *(Female, government, primary, metropolitan, NSW)*

Principal leadership

Four principals commented on their own leadership style, and the ways in which they influence improvement and change in relation to the implementation of school plans and policies.

> I try to avoid the authoritarian, dictatorial approach of telling everyone they have to do this ... You have to select the right strategy for the right setting, purpose and audience, so you need a collection of strategies. I use a research–plan–act–review–re-plan–re-research cycle that is meant to be collaborative with those who will be impacted and those who will be implementing. You need to have ownership, clarity in what you are trying to do, a sense of moral purpose to shape that, a sense of, 'How are we going to do it?', and 'How will we know that we have been effective?'
>
> *(Male, government, secondary, metropolitan, ACT)*

> I have a very pivotal role to play in implementation. I never make unilateral decisions. They are always done in consultation with my executive team. Thereafter, depending on what we are doing in the school, you have to gauge it by community sentiments ... [it's] important to have your community going with you, especially parents that are embracing it and onside. If not, then we have a problem.
>
> *(Male, independent, primary, metropolitan, NSW)*

Evidence and research

In answering Question 16, 6 principals referenced 'collecting evidence' and noted that drawing on research was integral to effective innovation, improvement and change.

> When we look at strategic decisions, and look at implementing new strategies or initiatives in the school, even innovation, I need to be confident of the impact it is going to have on learning, so evidence-based decisions are really important to me. It is not just following a whim or a bit of an idea ... [when] I'm not certain that it is going to have a positive impact on the learning of

> young people, we do a lot of research and evidence gathering before we implement our decision.
>
> *(Male, independent, P–12, metropolitan, QLD)*

> We did an 18-month self-study that covered philosophy, organisation and curriculum assessment, where we felt we were at the start of becoming an IB school and where we are now. All staff placed themselves on the continuum and then listed evidence that showed growth or the reasons why we are staying where we were. That was part of the evidence. In our Strategic Action Plan, we set the goals from the evidence we have gained in our student, parent and staff surveys, NAPLAN and AusVels. That hard data helps us set our goals and we can see if we have reached them and if so why and if not why. … at the start of the year, the leadership team set targets for each year level based on the cohort they have at that time. The other evidence is linked to assessment and moderation, and placing that against the standard that is set out by ACARA.
>
> *(Male, government, primary, metropolitan, VIC)*

Professional learning

Professional learning was seen by 6 principals as a key enabler of improvement, innovation and change, underlining, yet again, the crucial importance of this area.

> The other way of ensuring accountability and professional growth is having a very strategic plan around professional development. All aligned: Strategic plan, AIP [Annual Implementation Plan], personal growth areas, personal plans [and] data, and then booking the professional learning in, in advance.
>
> *(Male, government, primary, metropolitan, VIC)*

> We also hold ourselves closely accountable. We have a strong system of classroom walkthroughs which is a way of holding collective accountability to pedagogical approaches.
>
> *(Male, government, primary, metropolitan, ACT)*

> A healthy behaviour of reflection. After an event we will often have a reflective meeting, time for input, appraisal and recommendations. It is a healthy practice that our staff do; we would see that as part of our growth and improvement agenda.
>
> *(Male, independent, P–12, metropolitan, VIC)*

Student voice

Five principals mentioned the importance of student voice or input when it came to monitoring progress of their school plans and policies. They indicated that students were involved from the outset, identifying areas in need of innovation, improvement and change, and then having an opportunity to influence how the school would go about implementing those improvements. Student surveys about curriculum delivery and how students feel about the school were common strategies among these schools. Principals also commented on visiting classrooms to do a pulse check on student reaction to or level of engagement with new pedagogical processes and curriculum.

> We involve students at the first level, and then we have student representatives on our college council as well.
>
> *(Male, government, secondary, provincial, VIC)*

> Student voice is also an important part of evaluating policies and processes.
>
> *(Female, government, primary, provincial, NSW)*

> It is about privileging student voice. We did a great course through the Australian Institute of Educational Assessors on assessment of, for, through and by learning, and I did a case study, action research on students as self-assessors. I used my Year 12s because the things we are not good at assessing are the soft skills these young people need. We don't have valid reliable tools, so we don't measure them – and yet they are the most important things – team work, self-efficacy, problem solving, curiosity. How on earth do we measure those? They are at the heart of why we bring young people into our schools and pride ourselves on that … For me, it is the beginning of a journey, but I feel embracing young people as self-assessors of their own learning could be a real breakthrough, giving student voice far more agency in the way schools are run and managed rather than … setting up enterprise agreements based on factory models of learning.
>
> *(Female, Catholic, P–12, provincial, SA)*

School governance

School boards, school councils or governing bodies were referenced as having a key influence on the monitoring of school improvement, innovation and change in some schools. Five principals offered reflections on how their school boards or councils set or reviewed policy, and how that impacted on the leadership and management of the school.

> The connection between our school council, which ultimately is responsible for policy, but below that we separate out the level of leadership and middle management policies that need to go to school council and those that don't. We've got a number of policies that are probably more around operations and we separate those out. [The] school council doesn't necessarily see those and sign off on them because they're much more operational, but in terms of the key direction of the school, that always gets pushed up and worked through with the school council.
>
> *(Male, government, secondary, provincial, VIC)*

> Our board wanted us to become more familiar with business structures around strategies. We have a fresh plan around the key projects that we think will have the biggest impact in improving things in the school; that process has a number of check points where we can reflect and create data around our progress. We are trying a new way of implementing project ideas.
>
> *(Male, independent, P–12, metropolitan, NSW)*

Leadership teams

Nine principals reflected on the key role undertaken by their respective leadership teams.

> The accountability process used to be the principal goes to the board and tells them how things are going, and answers their questions. I now have a biannual meeting with the board and my whole leadership team where they share their results and present their successes and answer the board's questions. It works really well; shared leadership is shared accountability. It is a great strategy to check on how we are going with each of our areas and the other important part is that they are hearing about what is happening in other parts of the school.
>
> *(Male, government, secondary, metropolitan, WA)*

> The leadership team is … focused on, 'How does this align with the four key projects?' We have been using an in-house strategy where every person on the senior leadership team donates 30 per cent of their time to others on the team, deliberately collaborating with each other.
>
> *(Male, independent, P–12, metropolitan, NSW)*

> I have an annual conference two days offsite with the executive team where we look at last year's plan, set up next year's. We look at the school review and implement these [findings] in the plans.
>
> *(Male, government, secondary, metropolitan, ACT)*

Using data to measure impact

There were 37 principals – around three-quarters – who referred to the use of data as a key strategy for measuring impact. Their comments ranged from the use of data to identify areas that require explicit focus, to celebrate success, and to monitor changes or shifts in student learning or engagement.

NAPLAN data were often referred to with the common theme that principals see NAPLAN as being only one way to measure student learning, with multiple sources of data being necessary to judge overall success. Student, staff and parent surveys are used to facilitate consultation, monitor direction, measure achievement or success, modify a course of action or inform change, and to check on the status of a particular area. Attendance data, Year 12 results, satisfaction data and enrolment trends are common areas of measurement of success in schools.

> We have recently started to use the [Australian Council for Educational Research] National School Improvement Tool. As a school leadership team we ... determine where we are against each of those aspects of teaching and learning. We look at the NAPLAN data for the children who have left our school, and we look at patterns of data in Year 3 NAPLAN and in Year 5 NAPLAN, and then that helps inform ... our practice across preschool to Year 2. We look at our attendance data to see if there are patterns around particular children's non-attendance. We look at the demographics of our school community and who is choosing to enrol in our school, and why they are choosing to enrol in our school. We ask for feedback from our families that have left us at the end of Year 2 to determine what in their eyes has gone well in our school and what our areas for development are ... We also look at the Australian Early Developmental Index results to see where and how we might support young children before they come into our school.
>
> *(Female, government, primary, metropolitan, ACT)*

In terms of measurement, 3 principals referred to international accreditation through programs such as the International

Baccalaureate as effective in terms of measuring improvement, innovation and change.

Other measures and methods of gathering data included student and parent focus groups, building a culture of continuous improvement, use of data rooms or walls to illustrate progress, a focus on communication and listening, and consistently asking the question, 'How can we do better?'

School and system improvement, innovation and change

Question 17 offered principals the opportunity to add closing or additional comments about leading improvement, innovation and change either at the school or system level. Eight principals made additional comments on change, change management, the leadership of change, and setting the vision and purpose for change.

> Change is an interesting area. Unless you can be clear on why the change is necessary, then it may not be the right time for that change. Unless the staff can see why the change is necessary or how it is going to improve their work or student outcomes, then it may not be the right time. It comes back to staff, if you don't have the right people to lead the change, it is not going to work.
> *(Male, government, primary, metropolitan, VIC)*

> Engaging the whole school community in change is the only way to move it forward. If you don't have them all on board then you just don't get that positive impact.
> *(Female, government, primary, metropolitan, NSW)*

> For innovation, you have to build trust in your staff that you will let them fly with an idea, and that they know that there will be support there and it is welcomed. It is all about trust and having the idea, 'Can I give this a go?' I often ask the staff to give me the educational rationale in writing and explain what it is going to look like, then, we put things in place to support them. Leadership need to understand that, with any innovation and change, you need to ride the waves for a while. We had push back in the first few years with the introduction of the one-to-one device for all students. The other night we had a forum with parents, a third came, the others are comfortable with where we are going, and we talked all about technology and learning,

> not the devices. It shows you how far we have come. You have to ride them for a while, and be prepared to ride them, and be prepared to accept if it hasn't worked.
> *(Male, government, primary, metropolitan, VIC)*

> The notion of change excites me. I enjoy change and the challenge of it. I enjoy innovating and I get bored if I am not doing it. The day that I start feeling sick and tired of it, might be the day I leave. Not only do I enjoy the intellectual rigour, I enjoy pulling people with me in the journey. Sometimes the wrong train gets you to the right destination, you just have to be prepared to take the risk. Embrace risk and always be on your toes in order to survive.
> *(Male, independent, primary, metropolitan, NSW)*

> In [an] independent school setting, you need very good briefing of the board and the support of the school board. When you go through a change process, there are people who are going to get upset; you have to hold your nerve and stand firm, and you need to make sure the board is right behind you.
> *(Male, independent, P–12, metropolitan, VIC)*

> The best way to lead improvement, innovation and change is to identify the people who are hungry to do something, and work out what they need to take it to the next level.
> *(Female, government, primary, metropolitan, WA)*

'Giving back' and assisting others with change was also mentioned.

> I guess one of the things that I've felt over the last few years is I need to give back a little bit to the profession, and so I've taken on a number of roles – coaching roles [and] mentoring roles within the system itself, within the public education system – and I've found a great deal of enjoyment through that, even though it takes a lot of effort and energy. I've found a great deal of enjoyment working with colleagues either at the beginning of their careers or sometimes they're in the middle of their principalship, and they've hit a bit of a rocky patch and their director might have said, 'Look, I think you might need to participate in this particular program, you'll get a coach, you'll do this, you'll do that', and just seeing the development of colleagues. It was something that I didn't have in my early and mid-principalship, and I think it's just essential.
> *(Female, government, primary, provincial, NSW)*

Principals commented on the need to recognise the team effort that is required to lead improvement, innovation and change.

> Obviously I don't do it myself. I might come up with some ideas, but we have a distributed leadership model in the school. So, I have eight people on the leadership group ... every single one of them is reliable, and they have to give me a quarterly report on each of the areas – achievement, wellbeing, engagement ... and then, at the end of the year, they write me a statement of how they went against the annual implementation plan expectations, and normally they exceed what we've set out to do, which is quite challenging because we haven't set an easy task. So, I guess I'm just trying to stress the reliability of the teachers, their willingness to take risks, and their willingness to work extremely hard. There wouldn't be any of my regular classroom teachers who don't put in 50 hours, and they're not expected to do that, but they would put in at least 50 hours per week, which is 12 hours more than they're paid for.
>
> *(Male, government, primary, metropolitan, VIC)*

Principals also offered reflections on aspects of improvement, innovation and change at the system level. This included referencing a potential disconnect between what is happening in schools and system level expectations.

> Experienced principals need to be advocates for change within the system, not just within their school. In the first few years of your principalship, it is probably a bit too much to ask, but as you grow in experience, it is incumbent on you to improve the system and seek ... ways for the system to change. The research shows if you can bring it about across the community it will bring about greater change.
>
> *(Female, government, secondary, provincial, TAS)*

> System level is a whole different ball game, and around the political realm, and the capacity to influence senior politicians and bureaucrats of the breadth of what schools achieve, and the breadth of data that we should be looking at. Unfortunately, the political discourse is focused on literacy and numeracy scores on external tests like NAPLAN and PISA. In the school, the most important thing, in some ways, is to protect people from that, [to] develop a culture that doesn't allow cynicism of the political regime to drive what you do in schools, so people understand that data is very useful to us; it tells us

> what is working, it gives us a significant amount of intrinsic motivation and gratification for what we are doing.
>
> *(Male, government, secondary, metropolitan, NSW)*

Many principals commented on the importance of taking a staged approach to improvement, innovation and change, and that part of their role was to determine what needed to be prioritised for change to be effective and sustainable.

> You've got to do it steadily, like, you can't do everything all at once. Certainly here at our school we identified three areas where we needed to see improvement, and they were reading, writing and numeracy – probably no different from any other school. But, we took the one that we thought we'd have most success in initially, which was reading. We knew we were doing well in the early years. We needed to do better, but we also knew that we needed to focus on the consistency and the connectedness from one classroom to the other classroom, and then one year level to the other year level. Eighteen months into that journey, we then started to look and play around with writing. Eighteen months into that journey we started slowly on numeracy, and in numeracy we started with some of our teachers.
>
> *(Female, government, primary, metropolitan, QLD)*

> Constantly being mindful that while you are innovating and changing, you also need to keep the ship fairly steady. It is being mindful of the combination and trying to get that balance right between how much change to bring in. You can do it softly, softly and take it slowly, and it will take you five years, and I don't think you can work on assessment, reporting, pedagogy and curriculum in isolation, they are so interconnected, you have to be upfront with people about how it needs to work, looking forward. There was a time last August where I thought I might have tipped the balance for too much change because there was some push back, but then all of a sudden things started to fall into place and I was really happy. Having great assistant principals and [a] leading teacher really helped drive that process to good outcomes.
>
> *(Female, government, secondary, metropolitan, VIC)*

> Not too much all at once. We have lived through earthquake change. We need to progress well and progress in small steps toward what we want. In my school culture, it is a slowly, slowly approach, but keep at it. The water and the stone analogy. You just need to drip feed, make statements and check that what you think is happening is actually happening. So, getting teams

of teachers working together is vitally important for any change within my school. You get your drivers and initial up-takers to work with those who are a little reticent and reluctant to change.

(Female, government, primary, metropolitan, VIC)

Five principals questioned what is actually meant and understood by innovation.

For me, innovation is a word that gets thrown around a lot and I don't know that there is a shared understanding of what it actually means. Many people think it means technology or huge changes when it could mean that being innovative is making subtle changes.

(Male, government, primary, metropolitan, ACT)

Innovation – I don't see myself as an innovator, I don't have an original idea in my head! But I do think that the people I work with do and they really are experts. I do a lot of listening. I get the people around the table to talk; the expertise lies in people. I can use people's ideas and move things forward. I don't think I need to be the innovator; they are passionate about what they do. Innovation comes from the team – people working together.

(Female, government, secondary, metropolitan, QLD)

Conclusion

In concluding this exploration of leading school improvement, innovation and change, 7 principals reflected on their personal leadership style, and what impact that has had on leading improvement, innovation and change, as well as other pertinent comments.

To sum it up, a good leader is good at two things: creating a compelling vision for the future and what that looks like, and creating a culture of trust that will empower and equip people to give them a willingness to following you to realising that vision.

(Male, independent, P–12, metropolitan, QLD)

Too many principals try to find the rules that justify why they don't do things. Successful schools recognise that there are certain boundaries and know how to work to them, but not fall over the edge. I am a high-risk principal; I play near the boundary all the time. But I always know my financial position. I know the framework I need to operate in and where to cross it.

(Male, independent, P–12, metropolitan, SA)

In terms of leading improvement, innovation and change, a big part of any model that you look at it is how you develop leadership, or how you create the space or the people that step into the leadership roles, and you create the time and share it with the other staff. It doesn't necessarily mean they have a position that pays more, rather a title, and you create the time for them to do that – to have ideas and share them, develop the school culture and … innovation across the school.

(Female, government, P–12 combined, very remote, WA)

I tried to get involved in professional learning for myself in developing my capacity to be a more effective leader. It is important when you are leading a school to identify the next generation of school leaders. I like to give as many people as possible the opportunity to step out of their role so they see the different areas of the school.

(Female, government, primary, metropolitan, WA)

I think it is important that you don't work in isolation. I can't work in my own place in a bubble. It is important for me to network with other places, across systems and states, and even globally if [I] can. It is an important aspect of improvement, innovation and change, and allows you to have more creativity and strategic direction around it. One of the things about being a leader is not waiting. I don't rely on the system to introduce things to me to have a go at it. I think it is good if the system does, but [I] often think that systemic things are a bit slower off the mark. You need to be active as a learner and what is going to help your vision – knowing that and pursuing it. Being able to bring that back [to the school] and communicate it, and getting people on board and inspired, and having a stake in it.

(Female, Catholic, primary, metropolitan, SA)

CHAPTER 9
Leading the management of the school

Introduction
There were two questions in the interview schedule (see Appendix) devoted to exploring 'Leading the Management of the School', one of five aspects of the 'Professional Practices outlined in the Australian Professional Standard for Principals. The purpose of these questions, listed below by their number in the schedule, were to:
18. ask principals about the data management methods they employ to ensure staff and resources are efficiently organised to provide an effective and safe learning environment
19. enable participants to make further comments about leading the management of the school.

Data management methods employed to run an effective school
In answer to the question, 'What data management methods do you use to ensure staff and resources are efficiently organised to provide an effective and safe learning environment?', many principals highlighted the importance of management for running an effective school to enable teaching and learning.

Strategic planning and operations
There were 21 principals who spoke specifically of their role at a peak strategic operational level, ensuring an alignment between obtaining and the allocating of resources consistent with the school's strategic plan. There was a clear sense that effective strategic management and

making the 'right' decisions underpins instructional leadership, and what the principal and school are trying to achieve.

> Resource management is a big deal ... the multimillion dollar budget stuff is on my desk, but I generally do that out of school hours a lot – high-level negotiation with the department, but that is the business. If you have a board with a chief financial officer that would be their work. We are getting there, but it is not something for the faint hearted; it can put you under a high level of stress if you don't have financial certainty for your school.
> *(Male, government, secondary, metropolitan, ACT)*

> If you don't get the financial position right you are not going to be able to implement the plans. Very strong management and reporting [is needed]; making sure there are financial targets in place such as enrolment, staffing, costs, how much debt, interest on the debt, how much surplus is made annually, which can then be reinvested in the strategic plan.
> *(Male, independent, P–12, metropolitan, VIC)*

> One of the key questions I like to ask – a good leader is always good at asking the right questions – is, 'Why are we doing this? What value is it adding to our strategy, to our students and their learning? If it is not adding value, then why can't we improve it or grow it?' Just because we have done something for a number of years doesn't mean that it is relevant as we move into the future. So, it is aligning our strategies and resources to achieve our strategic goals and intents, which are always focused on the development of a young person.
> *(Male, independent, P–12, metropolitan, QLD)*

> The management is about the day to day, leading the management; it is always asking questions, 'Is this the best way of doing things or can we do it in a more efficient way?'
> *(Male, independent, P–12, metropolitan, VIC)*

> Comes from setting the priorities and directions of the school literacy, numeracy and pedagogy. Budget and resources need to line up with that.
> *(Female, government, secondary, metropolitan, QLD)*

> The main thing for managing it all is that it has to be connected to your vision and your priorities. No matter what area it is, [it is] based on what you want to achieve, and that aligns to the vision. All the things have to be

> strategically aligned. You have got to have your strategic plan, which ... all the management things come out of ...
>
> *(Female, Catholic, primary, metropolitan, SA)*

Clear systems and processes, and surrounding yourself with the right people

Twelve principals commented on the importance of having 'clear systems and processes', and 'role clarity'. These principals mentioned using timelines, checklists and policies, and that aligning leadership roles to the strategic plan was important. One referred to these processes as the 'operational things that have to happen to keep the school going.' There was agreement on the importance of effective systems that everyone understands and adheres to, and, once again, there were comments (n = 13) about the importance of having the 'right people' to fill management roles to support teaching and learning.

> We have really strong processes in place to deal with all the management, so it doesn't interfere with what we are doing. People have very clear roles and I have really good people around me.
>
> *(Female, government, secondary, provincial, TAS)*

> [School management] is increasingly taking more time than it's ever taken before, and you have to surround yourself with the right people to assist you to do that in order to do it well.
>
> *(Female, government, primary, provincial, NSW)*

> Leading the management of the school is fundamentally about recognising that there are many others who are better equipped to do it than you. You just have to invite them into that space and empower them. Maintaining, as principal, the responsibility of checking in or checking up without micromanaging. This balance is an important feature.
>
> *(Male, government, secondary, metropolitan, ACT)*

The importance of a good business manager

There were 12 principals (6 government, 2 Catholic, 4 independent) who spoke of the importance of an effective business manager. This role was once more common in non-government schools, but increasingly business managers are present in government schools as schools have assumed greater responsibility for certain functions previously provided by systems. Such roles enabled principals to concentrate more on instructional leadership.

Overall, it was apparent from comments by many principals throughout the study that schools of all types have become more complex and challenging to operate and lead.

> My previous business manager… I couldn't trust because she made so many mistakes and that made my job so much harder because she made lots of errors. So, my new business manager, she's fantastic and I don't have to feel anywhere near as stressed because I know that she doesn't make the same mistakes the previous one did because I've monitored that and everything's on board with that.
> *(Female, government, primary, metropolitan, VIC)*

> The business manager I inherited was an operational basket case, so we haven't had to do much to look good. The [present] business manager has done an enormous amount of work on improving systems and process, as such, the place is running enormously better than it was four years ago.
> *(Male, independent, P–12, metropolitan, VIC)*

> Our business manager is a member of our leadership team and she sits in on all our leadership stuff except when we're talking about the placement of teachers … But everything else, she has a big say in all of that.
> *(Male, government, primary, metropolitan, VIC)*

> You cannot lead a school unless you have a strong and robust relationship with your business manager.
> *(Female, Catholic, secondary, metropolitan, QLD)*

> In a school like this the relationship you have with your business manager is very close; everything you touch has financial implications. I work very closely with her, probably an area the staff don't see.
> *(Male, independent, primary, metropolitan, NSW)*

CHAPTER 9 : Leading the management of the school

> When you are looking at resources and effectiveness, I have used my business manager a lot. He is excellent at spreadsheets, analysing, looking at what is being taken up, utilised, underutilised, particularly in the last year, taking it back to staff and getting them to think about three things: greatest need, greatest benefit, weakest point.
>
> *(Male, independent, P–12, metropolitan, VIC)*

While having management expertise available to them was acknowledged as important by many principals, 7 principals spoke of the difficulties of this capability being limited in their smaller or remote schools.

> I have so many more people to rely on [in my present school], like the Infrastructure Manager, and the Business Manager knows her work so we can cut to the chase about strategy much faster than I found at my last school that had 470 kids as opposed to here where we have 1438. The economies of scale mean I can get to the strategy faster around leading the management of the school. There was less time for the real strategy around leading the management of the school at my last school.
>
> *(Female, government, secondary (girls), metropolitan, VIC)*

> In my own head, in our local area, there are three schools that if we worked better together we could probably share a human resource manager. If you are in a system school, you get that support, but there is a size that schools get to where they need one, but can't afford one.
>
> *(Female, Catholic, secondary, metropolitan, QLD)*

> I'm very fortunate that I have a wonderful team at the leadership level. It is essential that you are not by yourself. In some ways, I think we've got it wrong that we put our less experienced new principals in small schools on their own because they don't have the staff to rely on to do additional jobs and take some of the workload off them.
>
> *(Male, government, primary, metropolitan, VIC)*

> Coming from my last school, where we had few resources and I was much more hands on ... there was just not the personnel to help. I'm in a much bigger school that is really well resourced. It is a totally different ball game.
>
> *(Female, government, secondary (girls), metropolitan, VIC)*

> I came from a small rural school where I had to do a whole range of things myself, and now I'm in a very large school with capacity to delegate significantly, and so the role of the principal in those two settings is quite different. In one, you need to be really hands on, and you have a lot of time consumed with the transactional stuff and the doing, and in my role here it's much more strategic, and I've got time to be more strategic because I delegate responsibility for every function in the school out to other people.
>
> *(Male, government, senior secondary, provincial, VIC)*

Attempting to focus on core business through new roles

While 9 principals spoke of school management 'increasingly taking more time than it's ever taken before', 8 spoke about outsourcing or creating various roles and responsibilities to enable teachers and leaders to focus more on their core business.

> I now have a personal assistant who does everything, so I can be strategic and visible, and it costs me to have someone there, but I think it's a better use of money. It takes away some of the administration time activity that I don't need to be doing.
>
> *(Female, government, secondary, metropolitan, QLD)*

> Many schools have the daily absences of teachers managed by the deputy. Under the leadership of the deputy principal, we have promoted a smart individual to do that so that the leadership of the deputy is in teaching and learning, not in an administrative task.
>
> *(Male, government, secondary, metropolitan, ACT)*

> One of the things that has changed here over the last few years has been taking things away from the principal class and giving them more expert specialist roles. A big area, as an example of that, is facilities. That area of facilities management, OHS. Traditionally, in a school like ours, it was done by an assistant principal, but none of the principal team touch that now. That is recognition [that] it is an area of complexity, but in terms of the educational leadership space, it is not important; you can do that in other ways.
>
> *(Male, government, secondary, metropolitan, VIC)*

> Now we have a person who isn't a teacher, a person with high qualifications, and her main role is timetabling, daily organisation, and working with me in relation to facilities and a whole range of things like that. She has a

commerce background. She has a good understanding of money and all that sort of thing. We have quite a strong and very efficient admin staff. I think in most schools timetabling and all that sort of thing is done by an AP or similar. I think that's just a waste of money.

(Male, government, primary, metropolitan, VIC)

Including other stakeholders in management

Some principals commented on the role of various stakeholders including staff, students, school councils and advisory boards, and of 'giving them a voice in how resources are distributed', as well as providing 'feedback around resource provision'. Eleven principals spoke of the role of school councils, school boards and finance committees by mentioning the functional role of these groups in providing 'oversight', 'accountability' and the ability to 'monitor resources carefully'.

School council is a great governance model. We have a finance meeting every month. We have a great business manager who develops the financial reports, and we have taught each other and helped each other to analyse what the report is saying.

(Female, government, secondary girls, metropolitan, VIC)

Well, I think long before it was fashionable we were ... or I was, a fan of spreadsheets and sharing of the process for budgeting with whole-school staff, and publishing the budget through a finance committee, when that has not been the general practice in New South Wales public schools.

(Female, government, primary, provincial, NSW)

The school board is very actively involved in making sure the compliance aspect is followed with all of our auditing and our tracking.

(Female, government, secondary, metropolitan, ACT)

My board finance committee advises us on distribution of the budget. The leadership team will introduce a change that we want to make and, if we can afford it, they will support that.

(Male, Catholic, primary, provincial, VIC)

Being as transparent as possible, keeping specific minutes of the finance meetings so people can understand why decisions were made. That is all

> tabled at school council meetings and discussed again there. That oversight and accountability is built into those processes if you use them well.
> *(Female, government, secondary (girls), metropolitan, VIC)*

> The other area is my interaction with the school council. They provide feedback and they are the overarching authority. They P&F fundraise and 'friendraise', and it is a wonderful test for me about how things are going. They test the waters for me and will give me honest feedback about how things are being perceived in the community.
> *(Male, government, primary, metropolitan, VIC)*

While some principals (n=11) spoke of the positive role of school councils, boards and finance committees in being able to provide feedback and operate as an important aspect of governance, some cautioned on the power of these groups, and the necessity of having the right balance between advising and directing the principal.

> More and more, boards are [not] symbolic leaders within the school community, but functioning leaders within the school community. I don't think principals have quite got a handle on that yet.
> *(Male, government, secondary, metropolitan, WA)*

> In independent schools, the management is entirely effective if the relationship with your board is effective and the lines of demarcation are clear. The number of times you hear of a breakdown and it completely destroys a school if the board [doesn't] understand the difference between operational and strategic – they shackle them, they don't trust them, they impose restrictions. The management comes from the top, from the board down; if you think you are running these schools completely independently without that kind of input, you need to think again.
> *(Male, independent, primary, metropolitan, NSW)*

> I think the principal and the teachers should run the school. They're the people with the training and experience, and education. There's no justification for someone who's a dentist or a diesel mechanic or a hairdresser or a neurosurgeon to be involved in the policy making and running of a school ... the problem with having parent councils is that every parent is first and foremost wanting to advocate for their child, whereas the principal has to be an advocate for every child.
> *(Male, independent, P–12, provincial, VIC)*

The use of data in school management

Many principals mentioned that obtaining and using data assisted in evaluating how things were going at their school. Some spoke of a range of data sources being used to drive decision making and to assess 'where we sit and how well we're travelling'.

> The data for me is the proof about whether we are making an impact or not.
> *(Male, government, secondary, provincial, NSW)*

> So those data walls are very helpful for me because I can look very quickly, at a glance, where we might need to put in more support. So, in effect, what I'm really saying is, we use that numerical data, we use the anecdotal data, the stories that the teachers are saying.
> *(Female, government, primary, metropolitan, QLD)*

> I've been doing this for 17 years in three schools and the idea of bringing data in, rather than just professional judgement and anecdotal reports from people you trust in positions of responsibility. I rely on my own wisdom and judgment. I rely on those in positions of responsibility in key areas. I also rely on feedback from teachers, in particular, curriculum areas and that might be attending the English team meeting, for example. I also rely on external data like enrolment data or exit interview information, satisfaction surveys that are regularly done, SRC feedback and being transparent about what we get.
> *(Male, Catholic, secondary, metropolitan, ACT)*

> Data is critical. I justify everything in terms of data. A lot of our teacher professional learning has been focused on areas that have been poor and need improvement, based on what the data says. I can then also justify our expenditure in terms of that data; if we are not seeing improvement then that program is not implemented any more.
> *(Male, government, secondary, provincial, NSW)*

> Data for the learning analytics – to see how that is tracking, we use a dashboard system, and we can see how we are tracking against the strategic plan: three traffic lights. Growth of students is far more valuable than absolute achievement. HR statistics – in terms of number of hours of professional development, absentee days, staff turnover, those applying for lead teacher – enrolment, number of students leaving and why, future applications, waiting

> lists, and then, overlaying the enrolment piece, is a good analysis of your competitors and a good understanding of the catchment area.
> *(Male, independent, P–12, metropolitan, VIC)*

There were 22 principals who mentioned tools they used to assist with data management. Some spoke of specific data management systems, while others commented on data made available to schools through their state system.

> We have an online management system through which a lot of that data can be made available, so that teachers can get information about their classes or individual students. [This is] so they can have ownership of what they need to be doing in their own classroom.
> *(Male, government, secondary, metropolitan, VIC)*

> We pay money for a Somerset survey. We send our data to that and they send it back telling us if we are comparable, above or below other schools that would be considered similar to us, and we use that as a guide.
> *(Male, Catholic, P–12, provincial, SA)*

> When it comes to managing financial and human resources, our system here in the ACT does provide us with some great tools.
> *(Female, government, secondary, metropolitan, ACT)*

> We use a share point site to store our curriculum documentation; it is a resources site. Then there are system-based databases that we have to use as part of the departmental system. The data wall is a physical space. Behavioural referrals are all logged into the system.
> *(Female, government, secondary, provincial, TAS)*

> We are lucky that the department has a good online management tool for us to use.
> *(Male, government, K–10, metropolitan, WA)*

> It is reflected in the departmental data collection process. We use all that information to determine need and make informed decisions.
> *(Male, government, secondary, metropolitan, WA)*

> All my staff have been given access to all data that is held on student performance by the department. All staff are able to go through the portal, and access information about their class and class performance.
>
> *(Female, government, primary, metropolitan, WA)*

> We have to use the ACT directorate data management system called MAZE and everything goes on that. The Directorate are bringing out a new system. From a curriculum perspective, we use a system called Manage Back.
>
> *(Female, government, P–12, metropolitan, ACT)*

Professional learning of staff to use data

In speaking of the increased use of data in managing and leading the school, principals noted the need to upskill staff.

> I will send people on professional learning so they become skilled in interpreting data and pass that on to their peers. I also sit down with them on how to use the data effectively.
>
> *(Female, government, primary, metropolitan, WA)*

> I do professional learning to show them how to extract information about [a] particular performance on a test.
>
> *(Female, government, primary, metropolitan, WA)*

> They have been trained how to do the graphs and the data crunching themselves, and the whole staff have been trained on how to use the data effectively.
>
> *(Female, government, primary, metropolitan, VIC)*

> Reading and interpreting data is an area that needs further professional learning. Our teachers can access it, but when we share data you can tell with the body language that some have not used it before. They need professional learning around data interpretation [and] being comfortable in analysing the data.
>
> *(Male, government, secondary, metropolitan, WA)*

The need for better processes and access to data

Some principals (n=5) commented on the need for better processes around data management and access.

> While we get access to a range of data from the Department I think that we've gone backwards in that respect in the last five or six years. We used to get a very comprehensive school level report each year that was available in one document. And someone decided they'd put all of that online and in different formats, and it is really hard to analyse and digest.
>
> *(Male, government, senior secondary, provincial, VIC)*

> I think data is one of our big problems. It is like many things – we have three campuses over 500 km; two of our campuses don't have reliable networks or internet service, and our main one is spasmodic at best, so stuff for keeping and monitoring data is really difficult. Even attendance stuff is mostly coordinated by fax and done on an Excel spreadsheet. It is hardly 21st century and it makes things difficult to analyse. It is a real struggle for us … If you look at our NAPLAN results over the past few years, there is only one kid we have been able to track in the last three years. So, when people say have your NAPLAN results improved or gone backwards, well we wouldn't know. We don't have the information. We can't track if they have made improvements. We can get single snapshots … we laugh at doing NAPLAN online because we don't even have the internet capacity at two of our campuses to do that. They will bring their paperwork into the main campus and enter it there because at least the internet is more reliable on the main campus.
>
> *(Male, independent, secondary, very remote, NT)*

> Data management is huge and getting it stored in an accessible, congruent, consistent space is difficult. I have worked hard to align this. There is no perfect way to do it … If I could pull up one page for a child and see everything: interactions with parents, parent–teacher comments, reports, it would save us a lot of time. We are getting closer to that. As a staff we are getting better at understanding the data we have, and how we use it to plan our lessons and to improve children learning.
>
> *(Male, Catholic, primary, provincial, VIC)*

There is so much data available

Some principals spoke of 'drowning in data'.

> Data. Where do we start? There is so much of it. One of the things we have tried to do is break things down into manageable chunks for people to understand. Student achievement. We have always looked for at least three

CHAPTER 9 : Leading the management of the school

> pieces of data, so we can triangulate and paint a picture, whether it is in VCE, learning from Year 7 to 10. It is about agreeing on key pieces of information that we are going to collect and use, to understand the process.
>
> *(Male, government, secondary, metropolitan, VIC)*

> We are lucky to have a data management system which is superb. It tracks kids from kindergarten through to Year 12. It will show you quickly if a child is sliding or not. The data is there. The difficulty for me and staff is that there is too much data. We have mandatory reviews around classroom effectiveness, but we specify only this bit of data that is needed.
>
> *(Male, government, secondary, metropolitan, WA)*

A few challenged the use of more traditional measures of student achievement as a means of evaluating school outcomes.

> Data is something we are working on at the moment. We do use data, but not as complex or efficiently as some schools. We are not a data-driven school. Because it is a real tussle between what you value and what you measure, and how you measure what you value. What data do we want to collect? We have been wrestling with that for the last 12 months as well. We want students who are resilient, who have an entrepreneurial mindset, an ability to innovate and solve problems. And how do you collect that sort of data?
>
> *(Male, independent, P–12, metropolitan, QLD)*

> We have to continue to challenge it at the same time if we want to break the mould. What about the other 70 per cent of your students who are not engaged with ATAR? How do you give academic rigour, respect and what data do you use to analyse that? ... How do you allocate the resources to make sure your moral purpose is served? Deciding on measuring what matters; sometimes it is about measuring things that don't matter to you but matter to others.
>
> *(Male, government, secondary, metropolitan, ACT)*

> I think the overreliance, or the hysteria, generated by test results like PISA and NAPLAN is a good example of just how lacking in understanding these people are.
>
> *(Male, independent, P–12, provincial, VIC)*

Other comments about leading the management of the school

When asked if they had any further comments about leading the management of the school, 11 principals commented on the difficulty and importance of achieving the right balance between their leadership and management roles. In relation to this, 9 other principals spoke of the added complexities and pressures of autonomy, and increasing accountabilities being placed on schools as impacting on management and leadership.

Balancing management and leadership

> The management side is so important to enable the leadership to happen, but if we are not careful, the management takes over the leadership. The day-to-day compliance that we have to do, if we are approaching it in the right way and starting with the leadership things, will move forward. Having the vision and plan really clear before we get to the resourcing and management will enable us to line everything up with the right priorities.
> *(Female, government, primary, remote, WA)*

> One of the things I am challenged by is the role, now, of managerial leadership that we are expected to do. A lot of things that [are] low-level stuff and takes you away from core business. Things like requiring particular surveys are done – it takes you away from being the educational leader and locks you in an office rather than connecting with students and teachers, and observing teaching and learning. I see the importance of managerial leadership, but it should not be the focus of what school leadership is about. It is more heavily weighted.
> *(Male, government, secondary, metropolitan, WA)*

> It is a big job managing a school, but I consider it secondary to leading the school, and I mean leading in terms of teaching and learning, but I am aware that I have to manage the school well to affect the teaching and learning program.
> *(Female, government, secondary, provincial, TAS)*

Autonomy and increasing accountabilities

> There is one considerable danger in a heightened autonomy environment in [that there is] a lot of additional work for principals in regard to resource and HR management that comes with autonomy. Although it can be used as a lever for professional improvement, it can also be a major distraction from the instructional leadership piece that we really see ourselves in.
>
> *(Male, government, primary, metropolitan, ACT)*

> I think the ultimate answer in schools is to make them more autonomous and of course that will bring problems, and there will be schools where issues will develop, and sores will fester and then erupt, but that happens anyway, and I think you have to accept that no matter what system you implement there'll be weak spots, and there'll be disasters and there'll be things that will go wrong. Australia kind of seems to work on the principle that if you bring in enough regulations you will eliminate every problem, and that just is an unworkable proposition ... Just the regulations and bureaucracy, like I said, are overwhelmingly suffocating and add to the workload to a degree, which makes the job almost unsustainable.
>
> *(Male, independent, P–12, provincial, VIC)*

> On the outside of the school, we are governed by audits and inspections, and reports on the condition of the school, the use of the school, how many branches on the 286 trees in the school, a tree audit and an ember drop zone, water testing and audits on the pond. Regulation gone mad ... In the end, it is all about the wellbeing and safety of the students. Looking after them as well as everyone who is here on a daily basis.
>
> *(Male, government, secondary 7–10, metropolitan, ACT)*

> We do need formal process, absolute vigilance on things such as child protection, but at the end of the day there has to be a harmony between our structures, strategies, policies and systems so they are child centred, learner centred and we can have a flourishing community.
>
> *(Female, Catholic, P–12, provincial, SA)*

Conclusion

The complexity of managing a complex multimillion dollar organisation – 'I have a $7 million budget I have to manage' (*Male, government, K–10, metropolitan, WA*) – was acknowledged by principals. While many principals commented on the need to have a team around them to support operational processes within the school, the enormity of being the one charged with the final decision making, and ensuring their school ran effectively in an age of increasing accountability and responsibility, was noted.

Many principals spoke of the challenge inherent in their role of balancing managerial and leadership duties and goals, commenting that these were not mutually exclusive and that both were necessary for an effective school.

Principals drew on a range of roles, expertise, strategies and tools to ensure compliance and managerial tasks were completed, but saw it as important that these tasks didn't take them or their staff away from their core business of teaching and learning.

CHAPTER 10
Engaging and working with the community

Introduction
There were two questions in the interview schedule (see Appendix) devoted to exploring 'Engaging and Working with the Community', one of the five aspects of the 'Professional Practices' outlined in the Australian Professional Standard for Principals. The purpose of these questions, listed below by their number in the schedule, were to:
21. ask principals what they are working on with their school community, what strategies they are employing and how these are being implemented
22. invite principals to elaborate on engaging and working with their school's community.

The importance of community
Working in partnership with students, parents, carers and the wider community is a key aspect of this area of principal professional practice. This work involves recognising and understanding the many different facets that make up living in the Australian community including: reconciliation with Aboriginal peoples and Torres Strait Islanders, and their cultures; understanding and drawing on the nation's rich and diverse cultural and linguistic resources; and supporting families and communities facing complex challenges. The interview questions with principals were designed to unpack the complexity and depth of what community engagement means in the life of a school and the principal.

There was universal acknowledgement of the importance of community engagement, but it was deemed by several interviewees as 'really tricky', 'a really tough gig' and 'probably one of the most challenging areas of the principal standard'. This was reflected in comments about the amount of time that needed to be spent on building trusting relationships and networks in and outside the school setting.

Responses to the leading question, 'What are you working on with your school community?' indicated that a strong majority of the principals regarded community as a two-tier construct because they identified two layers of partnership, one with parents, the other with the wider community. A small number of principals also made specific reference to a third tier, students, as community partners.

Engagement with the parent community

Thirty-seven principals – around three-quarters – saw increasing parental involvement in the school as a top priority and the core focus of their current community engagement agenda.

Strategies for engagement

Twelve principals were able to report that the engagement strategies they had employed to date had been effective.

A key driver in improving engagement with parents was improving communication; there were frequent references made by interviewees to the effectiveness of streamlining and modernising communication tools and processes. One principal recalled that 'there used to be lots of negative comments online about the school'. He outlined how setting up Facebook and Twitter accounts, together with a parent link run by parents for each of the junior classes, was facilitating considerably improved communication and promoting a sense of celebration about school happenings. He recounted that there was now an active promotion of an open-door policy where parental issues and teacher–parent stresses received immediate attention, rather than being allowed to fester, which he believed was earning the school a reputation for 'actually taking action'.

At a simpler, but clearly effective level, another principal recognised the importance of visibility and accessibility to parents, and so maximised the opportunities for parental consultation:

> I am in the schoolyard every morning and every afternoon when I am here, and this is a great opportunity to be available, to hear concerns. More often

CHAPTER 10: Engaging and working with the community

> than not, it is a compliment of some sort – parents telling me what their [child's] teachers are doing well, or a comment on a school improvement we have made.
>
> *(Male, government, primary, metropolitan, VIC)*

In the above example and in other instances, a school's relatively small size was an obvious advantage for principals to communicate with parents. Other principals confirmed the importance and efficacy of day-to-day engagement with the community, noting how early awareness of parent concerns facilitated being able to 'nip problems in the bud'.

The desirability of updating and remaining in touch with the latest technology was a recurrent theme in the interviews. Several principals reported having enhanced parental engagement through the simple process of replacing traditional hard-copy newsletters with digital or online alternatives.

> Communication has to be through text, emails, phone calls; we have to shift in how we communicate with parents. Newsletters are on their way out, unless you can send it electronically to parents and it appears on their phone.
>
> *(Male, catholic, P–12, provincial, VIC)*

Technology was seen as a valuable and convenient tool for sharing 'good news', primarily to do with student achievement. One remote primary principal commented that:

> When students bring good work to the office we can post it on Facebook straight away while simultaneously ensuring that parents felt kept in the loop.
>
> *(Female, government, primary, remote, WA)*

Typical principal comments in this regard included:

> It's a PR exercise. It is making sure they know the good things that we are doing in our school.
>
> *(Female, government, primary, metropolitan, VIC)*

> It is about building trust and them seeing that they have a voice, and a place in decision making in the school, so they don't feel like they are wasting time.
>
> *(Male, government, secondary, provincial, NSW)*

Recognition that formerly standard school terminology might seem outdated and in need of revamping in the early twenty-first century convinced 1 metropolitan P–12 principal to re-brand his 'Parents and Friends Association' and attract higher parent attendances by hosting a more up-to-date series of 'Parent growth' evenings that examined issues such as mental health, drug education and alcohol use. The principal of a large, well-resourced school reported on the activities of an active alumni association, a timetable of guest speakers at workshops and seminars organised by the school council, and the implementation of recommendations from a triannual survey:

> Engagement with our community, parents first of all – we have good engagement ... They feel validated [through the survey], they feel consulted and included in the direction of the school.
> *(Female, Catholic, secondary, metropolitan, QLD)*

Several principals noted how the employment of a marketing and communications person to elicit and disseminate positive media coverage and promotion of the school has been part of a quasi-corporate makeover that has seen the development of 'memorandums of understanding' with all partners (including other schools and employer groups) and has reworked and reinvigorated the way parents interact with the school. As 1 principal commented:

> All our partnership agreements ... are being very clear about what it is we are expecting to come out of the deal. Parent partnerships, where parents are coming from: I talk with parents about their investment and what a success indicator will look like for them. I talk about parents as partners and have ... a documented plan ... [so] we can celebrate our successes. And parents change their vocabulary about the school; it has changed the way my parents talk to future parents.
> *(Male, government, secondary, metropolitan, WA)*

Parent engagement as a work in progress

For 18 of the principals, the task of parent engagement remained either a work in progress or a challenge, and in some cases a major challenge. One principal articulated a common sentiment lamenting the extent to which 'engaging and working with the parent community is fraught with difficulty'. Interviewees identified four areas they needed to address in creating improved parent engagement. These included: implementing educational change, parental involvement, cultural understanding and maintaining a cohesive school environment.

Implementing educational change

In regard to implementing educational change, 1 principal cited the 'fancy footwork' involved in:

> ... maintain[ing] a partnership when in some instances parents are saying, 'I can't fix it. You fix it.' Parents are demanding you do it their way as their way is the only way, and you need to respond in an individualised, personalised way, and at the same time get your community to understand the broad notion of community, and understand that moral purpose and what is the journey of change that we are looking to as we move from a conventional traditional paradigm into a twenty-first century one. That is a comprehensive challenge. And that they don't think you are playing guinea pig with their kids. Getting the message across that you act with purpose and that they are party to the change is important.
> *(Male, government, senior secondary, provincial, VIC)*

Another principal, working within an early childhood setting, recognised the need to shift what parents were used to being done in the past, and to share new learnings and approaches through class blogs and newsletters instead, so that parents were sufficiently informed to understand changes and they felt integral to decisions.

Time for parental involvement

Parents' lack of time was a significant factor cited by a number of principals across a variety of settings in regard to parental involvement:

> Parent involvement is low ... [they're] always too busy.
> *(Male, government, secondary, metropolitan, ACT)*

Principals acknowledged the financial and time constraints on families with two working parents or single parent families. They noted that it played out in a lack of volunteers for reading programs or canteen duty and an ongoing difficulty in getting school council representatives. In some instances, family financial distress came into play – 1 Catholic school principal reported having facilitated 100 fee remissions during a time of economic downturn. Within that context, successful strategies in lower socio-economic settings included ensuring that annual community events or school celebrations were free or low-cost.

On the reverse side of the coin, there was the pressure of multiple demands on the principal's time.

> [An] interesting tension for me, and I think [for] principals in general, is everyone wants a piece of you. More so if things are not going well. There is a constant need to makes sure you are accessible, visible, out there. In such a broad school it is not possible. You can't be seen at every single event as it is not physically possible. You need to work out the best way of connecting and engaging to maximise your effectiveness. I go to almost every school assembly every week, and I am seen at as many sporting events, musicals, kid related events [as possible].
> *(Male, independent, P–12, metropolitan, VIC)*

Another principal reported the need to:

> … drag myself along to public events, the musical, the band extravaganza, to present anything from chocolates to flowers to staff and community participants to acknowledge the work that they do.
> *(Male, government, secondary, metropolitan, ACT)*

Principals working in schools identified as socially disadvantaged, confirmed the pressures they faced dealing with issues related to generational poverty and family dysfunction. One principal recalled the personal pressure he had been under when an excessive part of his time was being spent in counselling parents in crisis; a pressure that was compounded by his own lack of training in that area. The solution was to employ a trained counsellor. As a result, stressful interactions between parents and principal had been 'significantly reduced' and, as an unanticipated by-product, the school had recorded an improved turn-out at parent–teacher interviews.

A number of interviewees cited examples of parental reluctance to engage with the school because of their own very different educational experiences, either at an earlier time in the evolution of the Australian classroom or within significantly different international or cultural settings. In regard to the former, a principal working in a socioeconomically depressed area of Tasmania admitted that building a positive and aspirational relationship with parents, many of whom were likely to have their own histories of bad school experiences, was her main challenge and 'the weakest area of my leadership and management' at their school. Simply getting the parents to come in to the school was 'problematic'. Accordingly, she noted that she was implementing the strategy of home group teachers ringing every parent and introducing themselves at the start of Term 1, and again at Easter. For parents accustomed to 'being summoned to school' only when their child was experiencing difficulties, she found that open afternoons coupled with a 'BBQ meet and greet' was having some impact by enabling reluctant parents the opportunity to celebrate their child's success.

Cultural understanding

Several principals reported the need for 'growing cultural understanding' about their parent community. In the context of the rapidly increasing diversity of student populations across the school sector, 1 principal pointed out how unfamiliar an open-door school policy could be to some sectors of the parent group, in this case recent arrivals from China.

> We are experiencing a cultural misunderstanding. [In] the schools that I visited in China, the boom gates come down for security at the gates of the school and the parents go off to work. It is taking us more and more time to make people feel welcome: 'We would love you at our art show' [and] 'Get involved in our carnival.' ... So, the notion of being involved and having a positive contribution to this school for your child is the key message.
>
> *(Male, government, primary, metropolitan, VIC)*

The above principal noted that his message of 'you need to and we want you to become involved' was making some headway in attracting parent volunteers, and that translating key documents into Chinese was helping.

> Chinese ... is the main core group where English is not the heritage language. We have a strong Indian group, but they can access English. We are now moving into using WeChat. The parents take the documents and put them

> into WeChat and translate those because that is a platform that our Chinese parents use.
>
> *(Male, government, primary, metropolitan, VIC)*

According to the principal at a small school in the Northern Territory, translating parent satisfaction surveys into the Pitjantjara language of Aboriginal people, and ensuring availability of interpreters at school council meetings, assisted with 'improving community voice'.

Another principal, with a high proportion of recently settled Islamic children, highlighted the need for engagement strategies to be sensitive and appropriate. The failure of a parent morning tea because no one on staff had realised the event would coincide with the festival of Ramadan, alerted school leadership to the imperative of heightening awareness of religious and cultural mores. Strategies aimed at making the community feel welcome have included inviting the local Iman to talk to the teachers, establishing a religious education program focusing on Christianity, Buddhism and Islam, and providing classroom space for a weekend Arabic school. The impact of this combination of responses has included an increase in parent helpers in class and in the carpark, and a very strong turn-out for a grandparents' event. Another primary school in a regional setting found that creating a community kitchen and community garden was helping to engage and build capacity in English for a cohort of refugee families that had previously been frightened of coming into classrooms because of traumatic educational experiences in their homeland.

One principal has worked to change the mindsets of parents 'who believe their place is outside the school and just hand their kids over', by strategically providing employment for local people as Education Support Officers, and by inviting Aboriginal elders and wildlife experts to speak and spend time with the students, and teach them about Aboriginal cultures, and lead singing sessions. The associated costs were significant but outweighed by the benefits. At the time of interview, the school's open-door policy was reinforced by the principal prioritising spending time to talk with parents each day, often about their personal lives, and by promoting student achievements through newsletters and whole-school celebrations. This had resulted in improved relationships throughout the town. Another principal of a metropolitan school with a large student population of Aboriginal peoples tackled parental reluctance to come into the school by visiting them at home and by utilising an Aboriginal Liaison Officer to survey parents on what they wanted for their children's education. In the process, parents were beginning to feel comfortable connecting with the school and this was helping change entrenched stereotypes surrounding parental non-engagement.

Maintaining a cohesive school environment

Ten principals reported varying levels of exasperation or concern at the impact on the school community of internal politics; specifically, the damage that disgruntled minorities, or as 1 principal termed them, 'rogue elements', could have on effective engagement with the parent community.

One primary principal highlighted the capacity of a small but vocal clique of discontented parents to affect morale and school culture adversely:

> About two or three years ago it all fell in a heap because of a few parents in my school [she recalled, noting that the situation changed only when] those particular people ... walked away because they couldn't get support.
> *(Female, government, primary, metropolitan, VIC)*

Another principal lamented the stress associated with parental allegations.

> ... accusations around bullying: 'We are pulling our child out because you have reprimanded them' ... teachers [are] not being able to build a relationship ... it is growing and keeps me awake at night.
> *(Male, Catholic, primary, provincial, VIC)*

The principal of a large independent metropolitan school recalled needing, as a newcomer, to tackle resentment, presumably from that sector of the parent community not happy with his appointment. He highlighted the success of a strategy of a series of community consultations, and open Q&A style forums where parents were able to voice complaints, opinions and so on. While sometimes challenging, the forums enabled him to gather useful information and for the parents to acknowledge they were being listened to. The principal in question noted how, on one hand, the consultations provided clarity around 'a mismatch between professional and parent views', a simple example was how early children were being dropped off at school, which was 'easy to fix but a really big deal for them'. On the other hand, cultivating the parent voice enabled him as a newcomer to 'dig with confidence' into claims of poor teaching. As a result, within two and a half years through promptly fixing a few minor problems, and through actively cultivating the most influential parents, who were 'the 10 per cent who turn up for meetings', the principal was able to report a turnaround, with 'almost no questions from parents coming from their own interests'.

In general, principals appeared to agree that countering negative parental input entailed improving communication and strategic relationship building. As 1 interviewee acknowledged:

> A strategy is only as good as the trusting relationship you have.
> *(Male, government, primary, metropolitan, ACT)*

Despite the majority of principals acknowledging the need for and value of community engagement, there was 1 principal who offered a strongly dissenting view.

> We feel, that as educators, we know what we're doing, and we have a particular philosophy and a particular style, and a particular way of operating which is spelt out very clearly to parents before they enrol their children here. And it therefore follows that, if they go ahead and enrol their children, they will support what we do and how we do it ... we basically just say this is what we do and this is why we do it, and if you don't like it, go somewhere else.
> *(Male, independent, P–12, provincial, VIC)*

The wider community

As noted earlier, as well as references to parents and students, there were also responses dealing with the broader community when it came to engagement: 'We don't exist in isolation, we exist in a group', observed the principal of an independent metropolitan primary school.

Another principal noted that:

> Good community partnerships are always about mutual benefit; if there is not benefit for both, there won't be a long-term commitment.
> *(Male, independent, secondary, metropolitan, SA)*

Acknowledgement of these sentiments and of the imperative of reciprocity in school–community relations seems to underpin most of the strategies reported by those interviewed. While much of the principal feedback detailed strategies to engage the parent community, around three-quarters of the cohort reported varying degrees of involvement or engagement with the broader community. These activities and strategies were quite varied, and included: liaison with other schools: sharing facilities, serving as a training base, encouraging community visitors, recruiting and employing people, staging community forums, partnering community groups, and getting to know and becoming known to local businesses and NGOs.

Liaison with other schools

Examples of liaison with other schools that principals mentioned were:
- cooperative ventures with neighbouring schools such as equipment sharing
- a six-school collaboration to stage a musical production
- a performing arts tour
- a project pairing secondary English students with aspiring writers in a local Grade 6, resulting in production of a book of stories and its presentation to the regional library
- participation in a sister schools program, teaming a primary school with schools in Western Australia and China
- participation in the International school-to-school program in Europe, USA and South-East Asia
- schools creating a FLO (Flexible Learning Option) catering to young people outside the education/training system, then providing active mentoring and support, including sharing its model of education and resources, with an independent specialist and welfare organisation set up in the same town.

One principal noted the following in light of the last point:

> The community needs to respond to this need [of providing for young people disengaged from mainstream schooling] … it's not just an issue for schools.
> *(Male, government, secondary, provincial, VIC)*

Sharing facilities
Examples of sharing facilities included:
- the school hosting a local swim group in the school pool
- making classroom space available for community functions, programs, language schools
- the school utilising community facilities, including gyms, arts spaces, university and TAFE grounds, labs, and lecture theatres.

Serving as a training base
Principals shared examples of their schools serving as training bases such as:
- providing further education courses as an RTO (such as IT mentoring for older people by students, or teacher aide certificates)
- facilitating practicum experience for university students in education and speech pathology
- reciprocally addressing university students about aspects of the profession.

Encouraging community visitors
Examples of principals encouraging community visitors included:
- members of parliament, representatives of local organisations (armed forces, fire brigade and police), community elders
- Year 10 students volunteering reciprocally with community services, ranger groups and so on.

Recruiting and employing people
Some principals recruited and employed people 'beyond the school's skill-set'. An example from a principal from an independent metropolitan secondary school was using marketers and business advisers with direct responsibility for promoting the school

communally, and creating pathways and opportunities for students and staff to connect with the wider community.

Staging community forums
Principals cited examples of community forums such as:
- asking prospective and current parents what they want from the school
- annual fetes and concerts, contributing time and people-power to communal fundraising events.

Partnering community groups
Examples of partnering with community groups included:
- local councils assisting in the improvement of school facilities
- engaging students in hands-on projects within the community.

Getting to know and becoming known to local businesses and NGOs
Principals got involved with and engaged with local businesses and NGOs. Some strategies included:
- setting up an 'Entrepreneurs Club' whereby local business-owners, parents and others, provide mentoring for young people on the premise that the job market is changing with great rapidity and that an estimated 50 per cent of jobs could disappear in the next two decades
- work experience placements for students.

The student community
A small number of principals made a specific reference to the student population as a community sector. For instance, the head of a senior secondary school catering for a transient student population from some 50 ethnic and educational backgrounds, described his school community as encompassing a cluster of sub-communities. In his view, the students were 'equal players', alongside the teacher community, parent community, business community and support networks (a diversity of government and independent agencies that support student welfare and vocational education).

Several principals saw the development of strategies to cater to students who were completely outside the school community as an important responsibility. One strategy involved establishment of a school annexe, utilising a building in the town and working across sectors to help transition adolescent students back to mainstream classes or to TAFE, university or work. The initiative was so successful that it was showcased by the Department of Education as one of half a dozen leading innovative learning programs in that state.

Other principals cited examples of students taking on leadership roles within the school such as coordinating a breakfast program for younger students. Other examples included ensuring there was student representation in the Parents and Friends Association, introducing student-led conferences, Year-10 volunteering with community facilities like the fire brigade or the local 'old folks home', and peer tutoring.

Conclusion

The responses from the interviewees strongly reflect the complexity and depth of the work that principals do to engage and work with their communities. The challenges that they faced differ with the many varied communities of which schools are a part, but overwhelmingly principals acknowledge that this is important work that they need to do to support their students and enhance their school communities. Very few principals saw themselves as separate from their broader community and as the only holders of wisdom in teaching and learning.

Most principals acknowledged that engaging with communities could be difficult, but their schools were enriched by the experience of working with students, parents and the wider community.

CHAPTER 11
Professional identity of the principal

Introduction
Questions of professional identity explore how principals understand who they are, how they should act, and how they see their role at work and in society. As identity involves recognition of the self in a role, and also recognition by others through the performance of that role, the purpose of these questions, listed below by their number in the schedule, was to:
22. give principals the chance to consider what they would like people to know about what it is like to be a principal
23. allow principals to reflect on what they wish they had known when they took the role, and what advice they would give a beginning principal
24. allow principals to reflect on any other comments they would like to make about being a principal or the principalship that might have been stimulated by taking part in the study.

To answer these questions the interviewees drew on examples from the five 'Professional Practices' outlined in the Australian Professional Standard for Principals that have been explored in previous chapters.

Being a principal
While repeated references were made to the complexity, demands and pressures of being a principal, there was almost universal agreement as to its rewards. At the heart of this was a sense of moral purpose – that education makes a difference to individuals and communities, now and in the future. Many interviewees also expressed having a moral purpose when they explained their motivations for becoming a principal (see Chapter 6). Being a principal was described as:

> One of the most meaningful roles a person can have in their life because they can make such a difference. They can make a difference for the children, the staff and the parents. It is such an influential role. It's a very important role and it is about that future – do you know together we create the future?
> *(Female, government, primary, metropolitan, QLD)*

> I think many people can be turned off being a principal because of what they hear in the media and what they hear just from their colleagues, and that's why I think it's important to know, 'Why am I doing it and why would I want to do it?' It's absolutely satisfying, but you almost need to talk to the right people to hear that. I think the right people are the people who know why they went into it and why they enjoy it whilst they're in it.
> *(Female, government, early childhood, metropolitan, ACT)*

Repeated references were made of the role being 'a privilege'. Overall, the principalship was variously described as a rewarding, challenging, valuable, enjoyable, complex, fulfilling and demanding role.

There was a recognition and belief that the rewards of the job ultimately outweighed its negatives. Comments included:

> There are the clichés. It is the best job in the world and some of the worst days imaginable. I think it is the most rewarding job you could ever do because there are so many elements to it, if you look at the complexity as a joy rather than a negative. You never stop learning in the job, so it is quite invigorating, and paradoxically, because you are learning all the time and you are a public figure, it is tiring.
> *(Male, independent, P–12, metro, VIC)*

> I love the job and the potential to have a fundamental effect on future generations.
> *(Male, government, secondary, metropolitan, WA)*

> There is no greater joy that an educator can have and no one does that for pay.
> *(Male, independent, secondary, metropolitan, SA)*

> Not as bad as it might seem often – huge joy, satisfaction in seeing success by kids and teachers – an honour, something worthy of respect.
> *(Female, Catholic, P–12, provincial, SA)*

There was, however, considerable concern over the pressures of the work that could, at times, outweigh the rewards of being a principal. There was a constant balancing act between managing accountability across the system, the community, the school, the parents and the students. Comments included:

> At the times when the job is at the optimum level of enjoyment, I don't believe you could get a better job. You are seeing growth of children right through to adulthood. At the other end ... it is a complex position where you can be caught between system, school and family expectations, and at times they don't align.
> *(Male, government, primary, metropolitan, VIC)*

> I think it's a much-maligned job. I think it's a fantastic job. Being a principal is an amazing privilege. It's an opportunity to make a difference, but the current demands of society are really putting pressure on the role because everyone's been to school, everyone's an expert, everyone's got an opinion and so the supports that I think the principals require are different to what they had in the past.
> *(Female, government, primary & pre-primary, metropolitan, NT)*

A number of principals spoke of the complexity of their work that includes many different stakeholders and increasing societal expectations. Comments included:

> The complexity of managing a people organisation; kids are not the issue, it is managing the staff and the parents.
> *(Male, government, secondary, provincial, NSW)*

> I think also, it's fair to say, that a lot of people have got expectations which are absolutely ridiculous of what a school can and can't achieve, and of what teachers can and can't do, and they only listen to one side of the equation.
> *(Male, government, primary, metropolitan, VIC)*

Other stressors from being the principal

Pervasiveness of the job

The pervasiveness of the job in the principal's life was described by many:

> The need to realise beforehand that it is more than a full-time job; it will take priority over family time, and so the principal needs to develop [the] ability to put the brake on – [it] can be really tricky ... If you're highly visible, it appears that you were just wandering around and being nice to people, which is the best part of the job, but you know if you prioritise that, and it is really important, you know you end up spending all of your other time doing all of the bits and pieces that are just there. You are the principal 24 hours a day, seven days a week.
> *(Female, government, primary, metropolitan, NSW)*

> It's ... a 24/7 job; you're always a principal and always on the job. People will see you down the street or the pub. I don't go there because I don't want to be targeted and I want my own private life. As a principal or teacher, people think they own you.
> *(Male, government, secondary, provincial, NSW)*

> It is the most wonderful job. It is rewarding watching kids grow but [there are] always two sides – lifestyle rather than career. Being principal is 24/7.
> *(Female, government, primary, metropolitan, VIC)*

> A real privilege – but [you] need to be able to let it go, balance [and] leave it behind when you go home. Turn off email at [the] weekend.
> *(Male, government, primary, metropolitan, VIC)*

> I wish that I'd known that it's important to really have another part of your life that you give to as you give time to being a principal because I haven't and many of my colleagues tell me that they haven't either.
> *(Female, government, early childhood, metropolitan, ACT)*

Loneliness

Some principals described the loneliness of the role:

> You are left in a situation where the buck really does stop with you, from a school level up and system down. When I ask for help, it is usually that it is up to me; it is quite lonely and intimidating.
> *(Female, government, primary, metropolitan, WA)*

> Loneliness of the job. You have your colleagues and peers to talk to, but, at the end of the day, a lot of pressure sits with you.
> *(Male, government, secondary, provincial, NSW)*

> It can be lonely, and you're certainly not in the job to make friends. You're there to make the best school and the best local community that you can, and the pressures that come with that can be extremely overwhelming from time to time.
>
> *(Female, government, early childhood, metropolitan, ACT)*

Lack of recognition

Some principals reflected on the general lack of role recognition:

> I wish the community acknowledged appropriately and respected the role far more than they currently do. I wish parents would know and understand that we're all on the same side, that there are no enemies, and that sometimes a principal has to make tough decisions, or they have to speak to their child, or they have to do things for compliance reasons that can't be undone or explained.
>
> *(Female, government, primary, provincial, NSW)*

Lack of system support

Some principals outlined the lack of system support:

> There are a lot of principals who struggle with that, and it's really taking a toll on their mental health because there hasn't been a lot of, I guess, support and professional learning for that coming in ... There are a lot of principal colleagues who are just treading water now hoping for the retirement age to come around.
>
> *(Female, government, primary, metropolitan, NSW)*

> Constant challenges to your authority – it is not about whatever I say goes, you are always second-guessing yourself: Am I going to be supported here? If I make this decision, what are the consequences? Whatever I do I have to think, Is someone going to appeal this? We are not treated as experts in our field. Anyone who has been to school is an expert. I wish I'd known. It took me a while to learn this. Your back is not necessarily covered and the support you think you are going to get in a larger system, doesn't necessarily exist. They often don't back you or support you, even when you are doing the right thing.
>
> *(Male, government, secondary, provincial, NSW)*

Lack of resources
Managing resources and not having enough of these was discussed:

> Not having the resources you need for what kids need ... I think ... a great many of us in the state system are deeply concerned with the continuing residualisation of our system.
> *(Male, government, secondary, provincial, VIC)*

> Being principal is more like running a company than a classroom. You have to make that adjustment out of the classroom into the boardroom. Underpaid in that regard. The finance and staffing is really something you would do if you were the head of McDonalds. It is not school or education related. There is talk about autonomy, but the more you talk about it, the more things tighten up.
> *(Male, government, secondary, metropolitan, ACT)*

Advice to the beginning principal
When asked what advice they would give beginning principals, the answers were focused on the need to develop support structures for the challenges that inevitably occur when being a principal.

Developing support structures
Advice on networks:

> Definitely join the Victorian Principals' Association and the Australian Principals' Federation ... get amongst like-minded folk. Attend every principals' meeting that is possible for you to go to because you'll form friendships and alliances, and you'll learn stuff that you can't learn by yourself because everyone's got a different set of experiences.
> *(Male, government, primary, metropolitan, VIC)*

Advice on mentors:

> Get a mentor. You must have a mentor. Someone you can trust, and not be frightened to ask any question of.
> *(Male, government, primary, metropolitan, VIC)*

> I wish I'd known to engage a mentor more ... I didn't have that when I first started.
>
> *(Female, government, secondary, metropolitan, ACT)*

Advice on having 'buddies':

> That there is no expectation that you know everything. I kind of made a few friends, and I would ring them and say I don't know how to do this, and they would be ... you know, it's like a secret principals' code – you know you phone a friend because there is no way that you can know everything about everything ... I think your colleagues are your best ally there, and if you don't have those networks I think you'll find ... [if] you don't go out and seek them, then you'll find the principal role really difficult.
>
> *(Male, government, primary, metropolitan, VIC)*

> Don't do everything yourself ... you can't. You need a buddy that you can just go and say, 'God, this is what's going on this week. I'm not coping.' You know, to have someone, a mentor or a good buddy, that you can just go and say, 'This week, I've had the worst week ever.'
>
> *(Female, government, primary, metropolitan, VIC)*

> Two groups of people to talk to. The first group of people, those who can give you information on the day-to-day tasks, what needs to happen – many principals I don't think ever had that ... Many of us have had to learn on the job. The second group [are] people that you feel comfortable with; debrief to them. You need to ask them questions: 'What do you think I'm doing wrong?', or 'What do you think I'm doing right?' ... people that you feel would give you feedback ... really listen ... [This approach is] underestimated ... don't feel you need [to know] all the answers all the time.
>
> *(Female, government, early childhood, metropolitan, ACT)*

The four other main areas of advice for new principals were: keeping the focus on teaching and learning, recognising the importance of relationships, understanding yourself as a leader, and focus on professional learning. These are discussed below.

A focus on teaching and learning

Comments in respect to focusing on teaching and learning included:

> Keep your eye on the prize ... that is, the student learning progression, and enjoy all of the good bits because they'll support you for the rest of the time.
> *(Female, government, primary, provincial, NSW)*

> Get your school running to the maximum level of efficiency and focus on student achievement because that's what will eventually get you the biscuits at the end of the day. If the children are learning, then the parents will be happy ... well most of them, not all of them, there's always someone who's unhappy about something, but you'll know you're doing your job effectively if the children are achieving ahead of where they should be, both in terms of the state averages and like-school groups.
> *(Male, government, primary, metropolitan, VIC)*

To assist with the focus on student achievement 1 principal noted that it is important to:

> Be really strong on staffing appointments. Do not renew a contract if they're a seven out of ten; they have to be an eight or a nine. You know, getting talented staff is number one.
> *(Male, government, primary, metropolitan, VIC)*

Relationships

Comments recognising the importance of relationships included:

> Enjoy the good times ... Schools are full of wonderful people, and we have to make sure we enjoy that and not get bogged down with sitting at the computer and attending to all the technical stuff.
> *(Male, government, primary, metropolitan, VIC)*

> Don't become a principal if you are not a people person; if you are not willing to admit you are wrong when you make a mistake, and move on and ensure you can work with people in the future because teaching and being a principal is all about relationships.
> *(Male, government, primary, metropolitan, VIC)*

> To spend time on the relationships is always what one needs to do, and not to worry if stuff isn't happening, like, you're not getting to email during the day or you're not answering that person's phone call.
> *(Female, government, primary, metropolitan, QLD)*

> You need people around you; you can't afford to try and do it all.
> *(Male, government, secondary, provincial, VIC)*

Understanding yourself as a leader

The advice on understanding your personal leadership skills included:

> You cannot keep everyone happy, so you've got to know what you yourself believe in – your beliefs and values. If I'd known some of the grief I was going to go through, I might not have put my hand up for the job perhaps. Recognition that I needed to be more self-aware – I was overly confident and had all the answers – I probably made life a bit harder than I needed to for some people.
> *(Male, government, secondary, provincial, VIC)*

> When I started I made some really big mistakes, so you need to be prepared to learn on [the] job and change your view. Take it on the chin if you make a mistake. The bottom line is what's best for the kids.
> *(Male, government, primary, metropolitan, VIC)*

> Believe in yourself and understand yourself.
> *(Male, independent, P–12, metropolitan, VIC)*

> Always be your better self.
> *(Male, independent, secondary, metropolitan, SA)*

> How to look after myself a bit better when things get really tough.
> *(Female, government, primary, provincial, NSW)*

> Mindset – remain calm, let nothing surprise you; anything can happen.
> *(Male, catholic, P–12, provincial, SA)*

Professional learning

The importance of professional learning was discussed:

> Learn as much as you can before you become a principal because you hit the ground running ... know yourself really well ... draw a line in the sand [and] do not step over when [you are] pushed. You need to sleep at night.
> *(Female, government, primary, metropolitan, VIC)*

> To keep learning themselves. I think education's a wonderful thing for the mind and that applies as equally to principals as it does to teachers, and so, therefore, they should, as a routine matter, make sure that they attend conferences run by principals and go to other learning opportunities.
> *(Male, government, primary, metropolitan, VIC)*

> Develop knowledge about systems; build leadership strengths.
> *(Female, government, primary, remote, WA)*

Conclusion

When discussing their roles and professional identity, the principals drew on the Standard's 'Professional Practices' to provide a framework for how they think about their role. In each of the areas of professional practice, they have experienced challenges and rewards.

Despite the challenges, the words of this principal sum up the feelings of the majority of interviewees:

> At the end of the day I do this because I want to make a difference, and I love teaching and learning ... For all the negatives I have mentioned, it is a fantastic job. The most rewarding job I have ever had. You can change people's lives, [and] impact and change a community. It is a thankless job, but one you can be proud of and say I did this with my staff and made a difference. It takes one person to say thank you, or acknowledge what you have done and it lifts your spirits. The benefits are amazing.
> *(Male, government, secondary, provincial, NSW).*

The principals who reported a strong positive identity as a principal overwhelmingly integrated the Standard's Leadership requirements, particularly Vision and values. They had a sense of moral purpose, with the focus and outcomes they wanted to achieve at an individual, school and community level. These principals focused on the provision of high-quality learning and teaching to ensure a generation of successful learners, happy fulfilled people and active, informed citizens, outcomes for Australian education articulated in the 'Declaration on Educational Goals for Young Australians'.[113]

PART C

OVERALL FINDINGS AND IMPLICATIONS OF THE 'I'M THE PRINCIPAL' PROJECT

CHAPTER 12
Overarching findings of the project

Introduction
We were privileged to engage with the 50 principals from across Australia who participated in this project. Their willingness to be interviewed at length and at depth, and the candour they exhibited, including experiences, insights and self-criticism, has provided a window into the world of the work of the principal today. Their responses also provide us with some evidence for better preparing, selecting, supporting and conceptualising the role in the future; these matters are taken up in the following and final chapter.

This chapter provides a bringing together of the overall findings of the project. These broad findings are presented using the framework of the interview schedule (Appendix) which, in turn, was based upon the Australian Professional Standard for Principals, as described in the methodology for the project outlined in Chapter 4.

Overview of the study findings
This overview of the study findings is presented using the framework of the five 'Professional Practices' outlined in the Standard. A final section of this summary presents data relating to the overarching concept of the professional identity of the principal.

Although there were some differences associated with the system, sector, size and location of the schools where these 50 principals lead their schools, overall there was far more commonality than not in the interview question responses.

Section 1 of the interview schedule: Leading teaching and learning

Reasons for becoming a principal

The interviewees frequently gave multiple reasons or factors responsible for them becoming a principal. However, these reasons were dominated by personal values, and wanting to make a difference for students and their communities (n=27).

Sixteen principals saw becoming a principal as a 'natural progression' in their journey of personal and professional development, while 18 principals cited the influence of mentors, role models and encouragement from others as being important. Having more 'positional power' and being able to 'make things happen' in schools was a factor in seeking the role by 14 principals.

Being 'always interested' in leadership was cited by 8 principals as a reason for becoming a principal, while 9 interviewees gave the influence of having experienced negative or poor examples of principals, coupled with a view that they could do better than these individuals, as a reason for seeking the role.

Six principals spoke of wanting to put into practice the skills and capabilities they had developed in schools over time in other positions, while 5 principals mentioned having had time out of schools in other occupations for a period as giving them valuable new skills and perspectives they were then able to bring to the role of principal.

There were 4 principals who spoke of having become 'bored' and no longer challenged by classroom teaching, while a further 4 principals said they had not been looking to take up the role until the opportunity had arisen. One principal said he had not thought of being a principal until, as an experienced teacher, he had taught Aboriginal students for the first time, something which had motivated him to seek the leadership of a school for Aboriginal peoples and Torres Straight Islanders in a remote area.

Reflections on capabilities for leading teaching and learning: most capable

More than two-thirds of principals (n=33) reported feeling most capable in the interpersonal areas of 'people leadership', and in building teams, coaching and mentoring staff.

Twenty-six principals saw their knowledge and understanding of the 'big picture' in education to be an area of high capability.

Twenty-three principals gave their personal vision and values, and their experience as a teacher and leader, as being areas of high capability for performing the role of principal.

Making strategic staff appointments, decision making and problem solving were noted by 22 principals as being areas where they felt they were most capable.

Eighteen principals spoke of their educational research knowledge, and ability to use evidence and data as being major areas of capability.

There were 12 principals who noted their capabilities of being an effective communicator and sharer of knowledge with others, while 11 principals spoke of their ability to shape and contribute to an effective school culture.

Reflections on capabilities for leading teaching and learning: least capable

As opposed to the mainly personal, interpersonal and strategic capabilities noted above, principals reported feeling least capable in being an instructional leader (n=16), and the related areas of keeping up with curriculum changes and developing curricula (n=14). Similarly, there were 10 principals who expressed dissatisfaction with being 'out of touch' through being removed from classrooms or not being as visible around the school as they wanted.

Dealing with difficult people (mainly staff and parents) and managing underperforming teachers were mentioned by 10 principals as an area where they felt least capable, while 9 principals mentioned their low capability to cope with the managerial pressures of the role.

Ten principals mentioned their lack of capability to maintain a suitable work–life balance, and 7 principals reported low capability in using evidence and data. Four principals reported a need for greater personal professional learning, but indicated that they did not have the time.

Overall, what emerged from the responses to the questions in this section was that a significant minority of the principals interviewed were finding it difficult to lead teaching and learning to their and others' expectations. This was because of their lack of certain capabilities related to keeping up with the changes in teaching and learning, and the managerial demands of the role.

Section 2 of the interview schedule: Developing self and others

Influences on capabilities, knowledge and skills required in the role

In terms of the influences on their development of the knowledge, capabilities and skills required to be a principal, the influence of others, and rich personal and interpersonal learning experiences dominated the responses. Clearly, based upon this sample, principals learn mostly from other principals in an experiential manner, rather than in a formal sense initiated and provided by employers or systems. As such, the process of developing the essential capabilities, knowledge and skills for the principalship, although rich and valuable, is somewhat ad hoc, informal and largely the result of chance or the goodwill and professionalism of others who are happy to share.

The major sources of such knowledge, capabilities and skills lay with mentors (n=31) for over two-thirds of the principals interviewed; professional learning (n=25) for half of those interviewed, and over a third with colleagues and professional networks (n=21).

The understanding of people and developing 'people skills' were noted as important by more than half of those interviewed (n=27).

Related to the above, learning and knowing how people learn, and learning about teaching and learning over one's career, were noted by 22 principals, while 19 principals reported they had developed their capabilities through working with and observing others, both 'good' and 'bad'.

Nineteen principals spoke of developing their knowledge of school operations through holding various roles and experiences. There were 14 principals who spoke of others encouraging and providing such leadership opportunities and experiences for them that were valuable prior to becoming a principal, while 13 interviewees reported the benefits of leadership learning experiences outside school settings. Similarly, 14 principals spoke of the benefits of having a wider perspective than that afforded by schools or education alone.

Professional learning and the role of the principal in the development of self and others

The essential role for professional learning, for themselves and others, ran through and across many of the interview question responses in the study. There was common recognition that professional learning was essential to school change and improvement. Almost two-thirds of those interviewed (n=29) described themselves as being a 'lead learner' or a role model as part of their fostering of a culture of learning in their school.

There were 22 principals who made comments about utilising performance management processes in their school – both the aspects of judgement and the development of teacher performance – as important in the learning of those they worked with.

Comments were also made about the importance for individuals and the whole to align professional learning with school goals, priorities and student needs. Some of the strategies used in facilitating professional learning included coaching, role review and clarification, use of professional standards and leadership profiles, sharing learning, distributing leadership, and building teams and capacity in others.

Remoteness was seen as a barrier or challenge for some principals, who felt distant from professional learning opportunities available to others in larger schools and centres.

Wellbeing of self

There was a wide range of perceived personal wellbeing from those interviewed with responses being, in effect, bimodal. Plainly, some principals feel they are coping reasonably well and others are not.

Less than half the principals interviewed (n=23) reported positive personal wellbeing and used terms such as 'happy', 'mentally strong' (n=5) and feeling 'generally okay' (n=18).

However, a similar proportion (n=23) reported feelings of stress and difficulties with coping. Dealing with role conflict and complexity were noted as problematic for personal wellbeing by 15 principals.

Principals (n=22) reported that interpersonal support from others such as family members, partners and colleagues was important in their coping with the pressures of the role.

Strategies to maintain personal wellbeing included periodic 'switching off' from the role, 'knowing the signs' that one is struggling, keeping fit and healthy, and 'leading by example', in terms of maintaining a healthy work–life balance. There was no mention, however, of accessing formal employer or system-provided support for coping with the workload and responsibilities of the principalship. Whether this might be the result of the lack of such services, or the reluctance of principals to admit the need for help, it is not possible to say from these data.

Attending to staff wellbeing

Overall, while principals talked positively about staff wellbeing and the structures in place in their schools to support staff, less than half (n=21) described staff wellbeing at their school as being 'good' or 'generally okay' at the time of interview. Although, it was noted by some principals (n=7) that the changing state of staff wellbeing was often dependent on personal and contextual circumstances, with some times of the school year or cycle being more pressured than others for principals and staff.

Strategies used to support staff included creating and supporting specific staff wellbeing roles, acknowledging staff achievement, providing relevant professional learning, being flexible and supportive of staff needs, and holding social events, celebrations and other activities.

Some principals acknowledged the benefits of a positive school culture for staff wellbeing.

Section 3 of the interview schedule: Leading improvement, innovation and change

Setting a vision for the school

In describing their vision for the school, a focus on and concern for the individual student and his or her future dominated the responses of principals.

Assisting students to be active, effective citizens, both locally and globally, was the most common response (n=18). 'Doing what's best for the child' (n=7), developing the 'whole child' for their future life (n=6), and improving the life chances of students (n=6) were other common responses.

A secondary series of responses was concerned with a vision for creating a professional learning community characterised by innovation, but, overall, a student-centred, global approach dominated principals' vision for their school.

The three big issues for your school in the next five years
When principals were asked to nominate the big three issues facing them and their school in the coming five years, the following responses were given. Each underpins, in some way, the improvement of teaching and learning:
- staffing for quality teaching (n=26)
- improving pedagogy/quality of teaching in the school (n=18)
- staff professional development (n=17)
- sustain growth through increasing enrolments, building programs, resourcing (n=15)
- building community partnerships, increasing parent engagement (n=12)
- technology for learning (n=11)
- mental health and wellbeing of staff and students (n=9)
- developing leadership in others (n=8)
- raising aspirations of students (n=5)
- better use of data (n=5).

Section 4 of the interview schedule: Leading the management of the school

Data management methods used to run an effective school
In respect of managing the school, the following methods, structures or strategies predominated in responses from those interviewed. There was a clear recognition that principals and schools need to 'get better' at using data and evidence, a concern noted in responses to other questions:
- the use of data for school management (n=22)
- strategic planning and operations (n=21)
- clear systems and processes; getting and using the right people (n=12)
- the importance of having a good business manager (n=12)
- school councils, boards, other stakeholders have an important role to play (n=11)
- focus on core business through creating new school roles (n=8)
- the need for better processes to access data (n=5).

There was also a recognition that despite a desired focus on instructional leadership and students, 'school management takes more time than ever before' (n=9), especially matters associated with mandatory requirements of systems and jurisdictions.

Section 5 of the interview schedule: Engaging and working with the community

Seen in two (or three) ways

There was almost universal agreement – only 1 dissenter in fact – that there were many benefits to flow from better engaging and working with the community, but it was also regarded as one of the most challenging aspects of the role, particularly because of the time necessary to build relationships and trust in and out of the school setting. Effective communication was seen as both challenging and essential in working with the community.

Community was mainly seen in two ways. The first and most important was engaging and working with parents. The second was engaging and working with the wider community served by the school.

There were, however, some principals who made comments about engaging better with students as part of this discussion, and seeing them as part of the community.

Increasing involvement: areas of success

There were 37 principals who directly referred to prioritising an increase of parental involvement. Strategies nominated included improved communication methods, adopting an open-door policy with parents and community members to improve accessibility to the school, principals trying to be more visible in and around the school, increasing the use of digital communication methods, better sharing of good news, use of alumni to advocate for the school, correcting misapprehensions and overcoming fears about coming to the school held by some parents, and creating new marketing and communication roles within the school.

Parent and community engagement a work in progress

There were 18 principals who described parental and community involvement as a difficult and ongoing challenge. Often these challenges were associated with language, cultural, and socio-economic issues and barriers.

In some school settings, many parents and community members have had negative experiences of their own schooling, and communication from the school was often left to negative or 'bad news' about their child's behaviour or performance, exacerbating their negative feelings and responses to the school. A challenge was to overcome such negativity and resistance. The principals provided extensive ideas and strategies they are currently using to overcome such difficulties and to open their school to the community for mutual benefit (see Chapter 10).

There were also 10 principals who expressed exasperation and concern over dealing with 'difficult', 'disruptive', and 'divisive' parents and community members.

Section 6 of the interview schedule: Professional identity of the principal

Reflections on being a principal

Professional identity is not explicit in the Australian Professional Standard for Principals, but it is a phenomenon that we were keen to explore in the study in terms of knowing more about the work of principals, how they feel about this work, and how they feel about themselves.

On the positive side, 47 principals spoke of the role as being the most 'meaningful', 'rewarding', 'challenging' and 'exciting' job to have and to do. Being a principal was seen as providing the opportunity to 'make a difference' through working with children, young people and families. It was described as the means to 'shape the future' and the world through education. In the responses, there was strong sense of pride in being a principal and in leading a school. There was also a strong sense of moral purpose – a part of the 'Vision and Values' aspect of the Standard's 'Leadership Requirements' – that gave the basis for why they were a principal, and this intention supplied assurance when they were faced with difficulties in the role.

However, while the reported positive aspects of being a principal far outweighed the negatives, there were comments that the managerial and accountability aspects of the role can be 'overwhelming' (n=5).

Some principals also commented on the 'loneliness' of leadership, the problems of dealing with difficult staff and parents, and the perceived lack of system support structures for principals. For these principals, the managerial nature of the work outweighed the meaning and reward that other principals identified as a protective factor.

Conclusion

The broad findings from the interviews reported in Part B have been brought together above and form something of an executive summary. In the final chapter we return to the literature on which the 'I'm the Principal' project was based to compare our study findings with what is known and accepted more generally about both educational leadership and the principalship more specifically.

We then turn to what our study findings might mean for principal preparation, selection, workload, support and development. We also consider community and perceptions of the role and the need for better understanding and regard for the work of principals today.

CHAPTER 13
Implications for the principalship: preparation, selection, workload, support and development

Introduction

In the early chapters of this book we considered: the general literature on leadership; the role and importance of the school principal; the qualities, capabilities and actions of successful principals; and what is known to be effective in terms of principal preparation, selection, support and development.

In a synthesis of the above, we concluded:

The findings outlined ... point towards principals and other educational leaders being most effective in respect of facilitating student outcomes when they have as their prime focus creating the conditions in which teachers can teach effectively and students can learn.

The most effective and successful principals maintain this central focus and uphold the belief that every student can learn. They have high expectations both for themselves and others. They are authoritative leaders, being both highly responsive and highly demanding of those they work with.

They realise the importance of classroom teaching, and the importance of promoting, supporting and participating in teacher learning and development to improve the quality of teaching in their school. They model the qualities they expect from others, including a commitment to their own professional development.

The management responsibilities of principals are significant and important, but the most effective principals find ways to deal with these whilst striving to be high impact instructional leaders. They are effective and strategic planners.

Principals must however, work with, for and through those who are engaged in teaching and supporting students on a daily basis, and thus professional and personal relationships are of great importance. Principals need to be able to motivate, communicate and work productively with a range of individuals, groups and bodies inside and outside the school.

The overall findings of the 'I'm the Principal' project resonate strongly and are highly congruent with the conclusion and synthesis in Chapter 2. The findings are also a shining light on what it means and what it is like to be a principal today. A key aspect referred to in our synthesis refers to the leadership versus management conundrum. While we noted in our synthesis that the most effective principals find ways to cope with that tension, our new data suggests we may have reached something of a tipping point. There are greater pressures for principals to be instructional leaders – and our interviewees say they want to take on and do this more effectively – but the growing management, non-core responsibilities, and mandatory compliance requirements on schools and principals are increasingly impacting on principals' capacity to be leaders of teaching and learning.

The discussion now examines the implications of the project's findings.

Implications for the principalship arising from the research findings

The implications arising from our study for the principalship will be considered under the following areas, in line with our original intentions, and augmented and modified by the project findings:

- promoting and celebrating the role of the principal
- principal preparation
- principal selection
- the workload of the principal
- principal support
- principal professional development
- working with parents and the community.

Promoting and celebrating the role of the principal

The principals interviewed were unanimous in their opinion of the importance of the role of the principal, and the potential they have to lead and develop teams of teachers and other staff, and through these people, to educate, develop and improve the life chances of students, work with and serve communities, and contribute to a better world.

All the principals appeared to derive great satisfaction and personal reward from the role, despite many having the desire to be even more effective. None interviewed gave any indication that they would not have become a principal if they had had their time over, nor did any express regret about taking on the role. In their advice to aspiring principals, none said they would attempt to discourage someone from taking up the position.

Only a small proportion of principals said they had harboured leadership ambitions earlier in their career; for most, preparation for the role of principalship was ad hoc, and the result of informal mentoring, encouragement, leadership experiences within and, in some cases, outside schools, and the role-modelling and encouragement provided by previous principals they had worked with and known.

All interviewed spoke of the rewards, excitement and challenges experienced as a principal, nevertheless, it is a fact that fewer people are being attracted to the role. This appears to be because of the complex and heavy workload and societal and systemic criticism and expectations, rather than the salary, with none mentioning the latter as a barrier to taking on the role.

There is more pressure than ever on principals to improve measured learning outcomes in their schools, and to promote and market the school, regardless of the system or sector. National and international reporting of student achievement and measures, such as compulsory reporting of school performance including the My School website (https://www.myschool.edu.au/), means that there is intense scrutiny of school performance today. In some cases, parents and the community are more demanding, not as understanding and less supportive of schools because they are more concerned with matters such as school status and their own child's wellbeing and results.

The social expectations placed on schools have increased commensurately with the greater attention given to academic performance – in effect, the 'basics' plus the 'extras' – and schools are expected to deal with the issues that society appears unwilling or unable to deal with. Whenever a social problem or issue comes to prominence, almost inevitably the immediate response is to hand responsibility to schools with the result being an overcrowded curriculum and a greater complexity of expectations, responsibilities and accountabilities.

Public schools, in particular, are increasingly expected, under the guise of autonomy – which is supposed to lead to greater flexibility and innovation – to take on greater responsibility for matters previously handled and supported by systems.

All these phenomena have two significant implications. First, they make the need for effective principals even greater so that these demands and expectations are met, and second, they may be deterring suitable people from taking up the role because it seems too big and complex to contemplate.

Consequently, it is necessary to make society and those who might be suited to the principalship more aware of what being a principal today entails, and of the personal fulfilment and impact a successful performance of the role can have on individual students and society generally.

Our principals thus need to be understood, valued, showcased, recognised, rewarded and their role celebrated. This needs to be broader and more encompassing than just giving awards and recognition for the 'best' principals. Promoting and celebrating principalship needs to be inclusive of all principals.

Principals have a role to play in this context in communicating what they are doing, why and how they are doing it, and what schools are achieving under their leadership. This is broader and deeper than external test results alone. Australia has some of the best teachers, principals and schools in the world, but this can be overlooked in discussions and dismay over such test scores.

Principals also have a crucial role to play in talent spotting and developing the next generation of school leaders and principals. The importance of these matters was recognised by principals in their interview responses.

Principal preparation

As noted in the project findings and above, the process of aspiring to and becoming a principal is fairly ad hoc; it is dependent on personal values, circumstances, interpersonal relationships, goodwill and opportunity.

There is a need for talent identification of potential principals and a more systematic process of preparation to augment what presently happens.

The introduction and application of the Australian Professional Standards for Teachers and the introduction of certification processes for teachers at the 'Highly Accomplished' and 'Lead' levels[114] of the Standards provides a mechanism for teacher development and recognition, and a pathway to the principalship. This is especially so if the Australian Professional Standard for Principals is utilised for principal preparation, selection, development and appraisal purposes. Together, the APST and the APSP would provide a useful career pathway from beginning teacher through to principal, although not all teachers will proceed past the mandatory "Graduate" "Proficient" levels of the APST and as yet there is no requirement for principals to have be certified using the APSP prior to or following appointment to the role. As discussed in earlier chapters, developmental work has been proceeding along these lines through bodies such as the Australian Institute for Teaching and School Leadership, Principals Australia Institute, and various jurisdictions and professional bodies. However, the full introduction of both standards, and associated processes of certification, coupled with integration into salary and career structures, has yet to occur.

There is a need for more formal and systematic preparation of principals, and the Australian Professional Standard for Principals should be utilised to guide and inform the process. Various jurisdictions have introduced leadership institutes to provide forms of leadership preparation, but there are currently no mandatory requirements or processes to become a principal in Australia, aside from the usual requirement of being a registered teacher.

Structured, formal principal preparation programs will increase the likelihood of principal success and need to be based on an assessment of the existing capabilities and potential of candidates, and on the broader knowledge and capabilities of candidates and their potential to develop the further capabilities needed to meet the demands of the role.

This is regardless of whether these preparation programs are mandatory and/or tied with certification against the Standard (both are advocated as a result of this project's findings). Experiential learning in different settings, educational and otherwise, with input from experienced principals and other specialist professionals, is considered essential to replicate and augment what we currently know works. This is rather than simply being content or knowledge based.

Such knowledge and capabilities, as revealed by the principals interviewed in the project, need to include:
- building and articulating personal and collective vision and values about teaching, learning, schooling and leadership
- instructional leadership: understanding and facilitating learning and teaching

- learning from good and bad leaders/leadership
- professional learning: being a lead learner; identifying and meeting the needs of teachers and the school; building a learning culture
- working with students: diversity, safety, respect, wellbeing
- current curriculum developments and requirements
- big-picture developments and issues in education and society
- strategic planning; using and gathering evidence and data; performance management for improvement
- leading and working with people: selecting staff, building teams, coaching and mentoring
- effective communication
- dealing with difficult people and managing underperforming staff
- school operations and management; meeting mandatory requirements
- using technology for learning, teaching and management
- building and maintaining a positive school culture and climate
- maintaining a suitable work–life balance; attending to wellbeing of self and others
- professional networks; supporting others in the role
- engaging and working with parents and the community; working with stakeholders.

In respect of the above, which admittedly is not exhaustive of the work of the principal, these matters were considered by those interviewed to be essential aspects of the role. They are areas where perceived self-capability varied widely. Hence the need for self-knowledge and having a personal professional learning program based on this self-assessment, and the assessment of those involved with the program. As noted, this learning needs to take place experientially – in schools and other relevant settings – and based on real world research, examples, case studies, scenarios and people. Principals in the study spoke highly of such personalised support and development, but such assistance needs to be provided more widely and consistently and not left to chance if we are to attract and prepare suitable people for this important role. The fact that a person might be performing well at their current level and in their current context is no guarantee they will be successful as a principal.

Principal selection

Some principal vacancies attract far more applicants than others. Some schools have a much smaller or larger pool of applicants due to such matters as socio-economic status, school reputation, the culture and ethos of the school, and geographic location.

However, to be led by the best and most suitable person available is in the interests of every school. Selection procedures for any position need to be rigorous, clearly defined, transparent, fair and defensible. These are matters for employers and are given aims for employment in all industries.

Of perhaps greater importance, over and above matters of procedure, is that those presenting for possible appointment as a principal have received appropriate preparation and met the requisite standards; hopefully they are certified as meeting the APSP as part of this process, have the relevant demonstrated leadership experience and accomplishment, and possess the qualities, vision and values to fit with and improve the culture of the school.

Promotion of the role of principal, talent identification and encouragement, thorough and appropriate preparation, and effective selection, as detailed earlier, are all essential to achieving the aim of an effective principal in every school.

The workload of the principal

There was a strong desire expressed in the project findings for principals to have more time and to be better equipped to be leaders of learning of staff and students within their schools.

However, apart from instructional leadership knowledge and capability, which by admittance of those interviewed did vary, the major hindrance to becoming an instructional leader was seen to be the managerial aspects and requirements of running a school. Some principals reported the managerial role of the principalship to be greater than ever before, with external mandatory compliance requirements likewise becoming increasingly onerous. In the case of the latter, too rapid change in these requirements was seen as problematic. These demands add to the workload and complexity of the expected role of the principal.

Some principals, especially of larger, more well-resourced schools, were able to shift some of their managerial responsibilities to other staff through creating new roles, such as school business managers. Others would like to do so if they could, but school size and resources are decisive factors in accomplishing such delegation.

The evidence from the 'I'm the Principal' project is supported by a recent survey of school leaders in the New South Wales government school system, which was released following the data collection and analysis of this project. The NSW public school study found that principals spend: only 30% of their time on leading teaching and learning; 9% on developing self and others; 6% on leading improvement, innovation and change; 40% on leading the management of the school; 11% on engaging and working with the community; and 3% of their time on other activities:[115]

> Analysis of direct observation data has revealed that principals are completing a high number of activities during the school day that are varied in nature and often short in duration. Principals on average undertook 45 activities during the observation period of the school day, with 28 of these activities being unique. 43% of the activities principals were observed undertaking took less than 5 minutes. Principals experience multiple interruptions during the school day, which makes it difficult to complete activities that require longer periods of time and attention. These tasks, therefore, are generally completed before or after school hours, in the evenings, or on weekends.
>
> Principals reported that they had reduced capacity to fulfil their role as educational leaders as they are spending a large proportion of time on activities that they classify as administration. Principals generally defined administration as all of the activities related to 'leading the management of the school' (comprising transactional and general administrative activities), as well as elements of strategic planning.
>
> The transactional and general administrative activities are often unplanned, ad hoc and variable in nature, and contribute to the disrupted pattern of the typical day of a principal during school hours.[116]

Previous work by Dinham[117] found that effective and successful principals strove to maintain a central focus on learning and teaching within their schools. They used measures such as delegation of certain managerial tasks to school administrative staff, creating new managerial support roles, and trying to be available during the school day for core business by undertaking some of the other more administrative tasks before and after school and at weekends.[118]

However, such approaches are not solutions to the problem of workload and work complexity, and are not sustainable. Employers and educational systems need to provide greater support for principals to be instructional leaders, and to increase the proportion of time and effort they devote to this by: providing more specialist administrative and managerial support to all schools; reducing onerous and counter-productive mandatory compliance and reporting requirements; and attending to the pace of change – mandated initiatives and priorities divert attention from core business and barely have time to be implemented before they are superseded by further change, as noted earlier.

In light of, and in support of, the above contention concerning the pace and nature of change, Viviane Robinson, a leading international expert on educational leadership, has recently published a book entitled *Reduce Change to Increase Improvement*[119], containing sound and timely advice for any school, educational system or government.

If a rethink and reworking of the workloads of principals cannot occur, however, then it seems inevitable that principals' capacity to be instructional leaders will decline and, in turn, it is likely that fewer aspiring principals will be attracted to the role. For those who do take up the role, stress, lowered wellbeing and poorer productivity are likely.

Principal support

The changes and improvements detailed earlier will go some way to better preparing principals, and easing and focusing their workload. However, principals will still require support, even if the earlier measures can be achieved.

There are two broad and interrelated areas where greater support for principals is needed, the first is personal, and the second more professional.

Less than half (n=23) of the 50 principals interviewed in the 'I'm the Principal' project reported positive personal wellbeing. However, an equal number reported feelings of stress. Both groups cited the importance of family members, partners and colleagues in dealing with the symptoms of stress; coping strategies included 'switching off', 'knowing the signs', and trying to keep fit and healthy. Overall, this support was self-initiated, interpersonal, non-systemic and did not address the factors leading to this stress, but rather were attempts to ameliorate the symptoms.

This study, and previous work cited earlier in this book, spoke of the potential loneliness of the position and the difficulties principals have in sharing with their staff, which could be construed as not coping or being up to the demands of the role. There is a strong argument to make attending to principal wellbeing more mainstream and accepted as part of the role. Principals need to be linked to experienced, sympathetic mentors, and there needs to be individual monitoring of principal satisfaction, motivation and mental health, with timely and suitable follow up. Reporting stress and asking for help should not be construed as a sign of weakness or inability to cope with the demands of the position. Employers, systems and principals' professional associations need to come together to ensure that principals have access to counselling, and other forms of support when and where it is needed.[120]

The second related area noted above is what could be termed professional support. Once again this needs to be tailored to the circumstances of the individual rather than being generic. Principals need experienced, suitable people they can go to confidentially for support and advice. This assistance might cover any of the gamut of areas that make up the principal's role, but two aspects that recur frequently in this and other studies concern working with difficult – and sometimes violent – people (students, staff, parents, system officials or community members) and managing underperforming staff.

Principals in more isolated schools have additional issues associated with lack of ready access to other principals and support services. They are also more likely to be less experienced. Efforts need to be made to ensure these principals are linked with others who can help, and to have the opportunity to have access to such people and, where needed, to have the opportunity to visit other schools and principals. Such arrangements need to be formalised and institutionalised, rather than left to chance. Every principal has a right to feel and be supported in their important and demanding role.

Principal professional development

Ideally, principals' professional development has begun well before they assume the role, as discussed earlier. Every principal needs a personal professional development plan. This assumes both self-assessment of needs and some form of external assessment or validation. It will also need to be contextually bound, taking into account the history, current culture, trends and the state of the school concerned. Formal mentors and support mechanisms can assist in the processes of identifying and meeting principals' personal and professional needs.

An important caveat with professional development, whether for teachers or principals, is the need for this learning to be evidence based. Teachers and principals need to be what Dinham has termed 'critical consumers of research', given that there are various ideological views, vested interests, 'quick fixes', and fads and fashions that plague education.[121]

A further point is that principals in this and other studies have reported a lack of time for their own professional learning because of the pressures of the job. Principals need and are entitled to periodic 'time out' to meet their professional learning needs as part of their personal professional learning plan. This could involve attending suitable courses, visiting other schools or other forms of learning. Principals sharing with one another, as noted previously, can form an important part of such learning.

Working with parents and the community

There was an overwhelming recognition from those interviewed in the project that there were many benefits that could flow from establishing and maintaining open communication and positive relations with a school's parent body and community. However, it was also acknowledged that this is not easy to accomplish and maintain, and that the relationship can at times, either with individuals or groups, be difficult.

As noted, learning how to establish and maintain these mutually beneficial relationships should form part of principals' preparation for the role, and their ongoing learning, and the support and advice they receive from others.

In the study, principals detailed a wide range of strategies they had either implemented or were attempting to introduce to enhance parent and community engagement. In some cases, schools had utilised new forms of digital communication, employed specialist people, or introduced measures such as surveys and focus groups with parents, community members, local businesses and, in some cases, students, to better appreciate needs and expectations, perceptions and beliefs about schools and education and to address these, where necessary.

Several principals described how parents, who had poor or negative experiences from their own education, were reluctant to engage with the school, and detailed how they were attempting to overcome the fear some people had about coming to the school, particularly when their experience involving their child had been limited to occasions when something had gone wrong and the child was in trouble. Principals were attempting to change these views through sharing good news and successes, and by showing that they are really listening to parents and the community.

Rather than reinventing of wheels there is sense in sharing these examples of effective practice in parent and community engagement across the profession, especially strategies that have proved successful in more challenging educational settings.

Conclusion

In the 'I'm the Principal' project and this book, we have attempted to shed light on the processes of becoming a principal, what it takes to be a principal, what principals do, what they value and feel, and what they need, in performing their vital role in influencing and informing the lives of individuals, the community, and society more generally.

This knowledge and understanding, gained from the experiences and insights of those interviewed as part of the project, is valuable because, quite simply, there has never been so much pressure and such high expectations on schools as there is today; principals lead this crucial and highly scrutinised work of educating our young people now and into the future.

We need better understanding and rethinking of the role of the principal if schools are to have any chance of delivering on the varied and complex expectations society sets for them.

We hope that in undertaking this project and sharing the knowledge we have gained through it, that we have added to this collective knowledge and understanding of the work of the principal, and contributed to an evidence base for rethinking, reshaping and better supporting the role into the future.

Notes

1. Chapters 1, 2 and 3 draw heavily on S Dinham, *Leading learning and teaching*, ACER Press, Melbourne, 2016.
2. National Association of Secondary School Principals, *Leadership matters: what the research says about the importance of school leadership*, NASSP, Alexandria, VA, 2013, p. 2.
3. S Dinham, op. cit., pp. 133–5.
4. An internet search of 'principal' and 'leadership' will yield over 280 million hits.
5. This section is drawn from S Dinham, op. cit., Chapter 9.
6. P Northouse, *Leadership*, 4th edn, Sage, Thousand Oaks, CA, 2007, p. 2.
7. P Northouse, ibid., p. 3.
8. See P Gronn, 'Distributed leadership', in K Leithwood & P Hallinger (eds), *Second international handbook of educational leadership and administration*, Kluwer Academic Publishers, Dordrecht, Netherlands, 2002, pp. 653–96.
9. Cited in P Northouse, op. cit., p. 8.
10. F English, 'Introduction: a metadiscursive perspective on the landscape of educational leadership in the 21st century', in F English (ed.), *The Sage handbook of educational leadership*, Sage Publications, Thousand Oaks, CA, 2005, pp. xi–xii.
11. J Kotterman, 'Leadership versus management: what's the difference?', *The Journal for Quality and Participation*, vol. 29, no. 2, 2006, pp. 13–17. Reprinted with permission from Journal for Quality and Participation © 2006 ASQ, www.asq.org
12. ibid., p. 16.
13. J Kotter, *A force for change: how leadership differs from management*, Free Press, New York, 1990, pp. 3–8.
14. M Weber, *The Protestant ethic and the spirit of capitalism*, trans. T Parsons, 1930, Allen & Unwin, London, 1905.
15. Today the words 'bureaucracy' and 'bureaucrat' are often considered to be pejoratives, but in Weber's conception, they emphasised objectivity, and that there are rules and processes to govern the behaviour of all within the organisation.
16. This section is drawn from S Dinham, op. cit., Chapter 10.

17 For example see S Davis, L Darling-Hammond, M LaPointe & D Meyerson, *School leadership study: developing successful principals* (Review of Research), Stanford Educational Leadership Institute, Stanford University, CA, 2005.

18 The following are examples of this: M Barber, F Whelan & M Clark, *Capturing the leadership premium: how the world's top school systems are building leadership capacity for the future*, McKinsey & Company, New York, 2010; C Day, P Sammons, D Hopkins, A Harris, K Leithwood, Q Gu, E Brown, E Ahtaridou & A Kington, *The Impact of school leadership on pupil outcomes: final report*, UK department for children, schools and families, Nottingham, 2009; K Leithwood, S Patten & D Jantzi, 'Testing a conception of how school leadership influences student learning', *Educational Administration Quarterly*, vol. 46, no. 5, 2010, pp. 671–706; A Schleicher (ed.), *Preparing teachers and developing school leaders for the 21st century: lessons from around the world*, OECD Publishing, Paris, 2012; and K Wahlstrom, 'Leadership and learning: what these articles tell us', *Educational Administration Quarterly*, vol. 44, no. 4, 2008, pp. 593–7.

19 Australian Institute for Teaching and School Leadership, *Australian professional standard for principals and the leadership profiles*, AITSL, Melbourne, 2014.

20 K Leithwood, D Jantzi & R Steinbach, 'Leadership practices for accountable schools' in K Leithwood & P Hallinger (eds.), op. cit., pp. 849–79; S Dinham, P Collarbone, M Evans & A Mackay, 'The development and proposed use of a national standard for principals in Australia', *Educational Management, Administration and Leadership*, vol. 41, no. 4, 2013, pp. 466–82.

21 A Harris (ed.), *Distributed school leadership: different perspectives*, Springer Press, London, 2009.

22 J Hattie, *Visible learning – a synthesis of over 800 meta-analyses relating to achievement*, Routledge, London, 2009, p. 83.

23 S Wright, S Horn & W Sanders, 'Teacher and classroom context effects on student achievement: implications for teacher evaluation', *Journal of Personnel Evaluation in Education*, vol. 11, 1997, pp. 57–67.

24 K Wahlstrom & K Seashore Louis, 'How teachers experience principal leadership: the roles of professional community, trust, efficacy, and shared responsibility', *Educational Administration Quarterly*, vol. 44, no. 4, 2008, pp. 458–95, p. 459.

25 J Hattie, (2012), *Visible learning for teachers*, Routledge, 2012, p. 252.

26 S Dinham, *How to get your school moving and improving: an evidence-based approach*, ACER Press, Melbourne, 2008, p. 15.

27 R Marzano, T Waters & B McNulty, *School leadership that works: from research to results*, Association for Supervision and Curriculum Development (ASCD), Alexandria, US, 2005, pp. 10–12.

28 V Robinson, C Lloyd & K Rowe, 'The impact of leadership on student outcomes: an analysis of the differential effects of leadership types', *Educational Administration Quarterly*, vol. 44, 2008, pp. 635–74, p. 638.

29 P Hallinger, 'Instructional leadership and the school principal: a passing fancy that refuses to fade away', *Leadership and Policy in Schools*, vol. 4, 2005, pp. 221–39.

30 ibid., p. 228.

31 V Robinson et al., ,2008, op. cit., p. 639.

32 See S Dinham, 'Restructuring: the myths, the realities and survival', *The Practising Administrator*, vol. 20, no.3, 1998, pp. 4–5, 51.

33 S Dinham & K Rowe, *Teaching and learning in middle schooling: a review of the literature; a report to the New Zealand Ministry of Education*, ACER Press, Melbourne, 2007; J Hattie, 2009, op. cit.

34 V Robinson, C Lloyd, & K Rowe, op. cit., 2008, p. 666.

35 See also G Chase & M Kane, *The principal as instructional leader: how much more time before we act?*, Education Commission of the States, Denver, 1983.

36 See M Barber & M Mourshed, *How the world's best-performing school systems come out on top*, McKinsey and Company, New York, 2007.

37 Exhibit from *How the world's best-performing school systems come out on top*, Sept 2007, p. 7, McKinsey & Company, www.mckinsey.com. Copyright © 2018 McKinsey & Company. All rights reserved. Reprinted by permission.

38 ibid., p. 28.

39 K Leithwood, K Seashore Louis, S Anderson & K Wahlstrom, *Review of research: how leadership influences student learning*, The Wallace Foundation, New York, 2004, p. 5.

40 S Dinham, 'Principal leadership for outstanding educational outcomes', *Journal of Educational Administration*, vol. 43, no. 4, pp. 338–56, 2005, p. 340; quote from Sergiovanni from T Sergiovanni, *The principalship: a reflective practice perspective*, 3rd edn, Allyn & Bacon, Boston, MA, 1995, p. 83.

41 See R O Owens, *Organizational behavior in education: adaptive leadership and school reform*, 8th edn, Pearson, Boston, MA, 2004, p. 259.

42 S Dinham, 2005, op. cit., pp. 340–1.

43 Ministerial Council on Education, Employment, Training and Youth Affairs, *Melbourne declaration on educational goals for young Australians*. MCEETYA, Canberra, 2008.

44 The Wallace Foundation, *The principal as leader: guiding schools to better teaching and learning*, the Wallace Foundation, New York, 2013, p. 6.

45 S Dinham, 2005, op. cit., pp. 343–54, 340.

46 Office for Standards in Education, *Children's Services and Skills*. See https://www.gov.uk/government/organisations/ofsted/about

47 P Matthews, *How do school leaders successfully lead learning?*, P Lewis (ed.), National College for School Leadership, Nottingham, n.d, http://dera.ioe.ac.uk/, viewed 2 February 2018.

48 ibid., p. 9.

49 ibid., p. 38.

50 C Day et al., op. cit.

51 ibid., p. 1.

52 ibid., pp. x–xvii.

53 V Robinson, M Hohepa & C Lloyd, School leadership and student outcomes: identifying what works and why, New Zealand Ministry of Education,

Wellington, New Zealand, 2009, https://www.educationcounts.govt.nz/__data/assets/pdf_file/0017/60182/Chapter-1-Executive-Summary-redacted-2015.pdf, viewed 18 May, 2018. Available under a Creative Commons Attribution 4.0 International (CC BY 4.0). Full terms at https://creativecommons.org/licenses/by/4.0/.

54 See also V Robinson et al., 2008, op. cit.
55 Robinson, et al., 2009. p. 40.
56 ibid., p. 39.
57 S Dinham, 'How schools get moving and keep improving: leadership for teacher learning, student success and school renewal', *Australian Journal of Education*, vol. 51, no. 3, 2007a, pp. 263–75.
58 L Darling-Hammond, M LaPointe, D Meyerson & M Orr, *Preparing school leaders for a changing world: lessons from exemplary leadership development programs*. School leadership study: executive summary, Stanford Educational Leadership Institute, commissioned by the Wallace Foundation, Stanford University, CA, 2007a, http://www.wallacefoundation.org, viewed 5 February 2018, p. ii.
59 L Darling-Hammond, M LaPointe, D Meyerson, M Orr & C Cohen, *Preparing school leaders for a changing world: lessons from exemplary leadership development programs*. School leadership study: final report, Stanford Educational Leadership Institute, commissioned by the Wallace Foundation, Stanford University, CA, 2007b, http://www.wallacefoundation.org, viewed 5 February 2018.
60 Darling-Hammond et al., 2007a, op. cit., p. 6.
61 ibid., pp. 7, 9.
62 ibid., p. 9.
63 ibid., p. 10.
64 © 2017 Australian Institute for Teaching and School Leadership (AITSL). *Preparing Future Leaders – Effective preparation for aspiring school principals*, AITSL, Melbourne, 2015, http://www.aitsl.edu.au/, viewed 5 February 2018, pp. 1–3.
65 See L Ingvarson, M Anderson, P Gronn & A Jackson, *Standards for school leadership: a critical review of the literature*, Teaching Australia, Canberra, 2006; Interstate School Leaders Licensure Consortium, *Interstate School Leaders Licensure Consortium: standards for school leaders*, Council of Chief State School Officers, Washington, DC, 1996; quoted content from: K Christie, B Thompson & G Whiteley, *Strong leaders, strong achievement: model policy for producing the leaders to drive student success*, Education Commission of the States, Denver, CO, 2009, p. 1.
66 N Dempster, *The professional development of school principals: a fine balance*, Griffith University, Queensland, Griffith University Public Lecture Series, Professorial Lecture, 24 May, 2001, p. 18.
67 L Ingvarson et al., op. cit.; S Clarke, 'Only connect: Australia's recent attempts to forge a national agenda for quality school leadership', in M Brundrett & M Crawford (eds), *Developing school leaders: an international perspective*, Routledge, London, 2008, pp. 138–54.; S Dinham, L Ingvarson & E Kleinhenz, 'Investing in teacher quality: doing what matters most', in *Teaching talent: the best teachers for Australia's classrooms*, Business Council of Australia, Melbourne, 2008a.

68 M Anderson, P Gronn, L Ingvarson, A Jackson, E Kleinhenz, P McKenzie, B Mulford & N Thornton, *OECD improving school leadership activity: Australia – country background report*. A report prepared for the Australian Government Department of Education, Science and Training by Australian Council for Educational Research (ACER), Department of Education, Employment and Workplace Relation (DEEWR), Canberra, 2007, p. 58. To note that certification of principals against the Australian Professional Standard for Principals has been proposed, but how and when this might be implemented, and whether it would be mandatory prior to or after appointment, or optional, is not known at the time of writing.

69 Darling-Hammond et al., op. cit.

70 Hay Group. (2010). *Aspiring Principals Final Report*. Melbourne: Australian Institute for Teaching and School Leadership.

71 Hay Group. (2010), pp. 14–15.

72 Hay Group. (2010), p. 15.

73 Drummond, K. (2008). *Future leaders: Fostering and developing emerging and aspiring leaders at the workplace level*. Sydney: NSW Department of Education and Training.

74 Hay Group. (2010), p. 7.

75 An online search using 'principal selection' as the key words will yield over half a billion hits, over a million of which are videos. The field is plainly enormous.

76 Council of Chief State School Officers, *Educational leadership policy standards: ISLLC 2008*, Council of Chief State School Officers, Washington, DC, 2008. http://education.ky.gov/districts/SBDM/Documents/SBDM_Prin-Sel-Guide.pdf

77 Kentucky Department of Education, *SBDM Selecting a principal guidebook*, Kentucky Department of Education, Kentucky, 2015. http://education.ky.gov/districts/SBDM/Documents/SBDM_Prin-Sel-Guide.pdf

78 See S Dinham, L Ingvarson, E Kleinhenz & M Anderson, *The draft national professional standards framework for teachers and school leaders*, ACER Press, Melbourne, 2009; S Dinham et al., 2013, op. cit.

79 Australian Institute for Teaching and School Leadership, 2014, op. cit.; S Dinham et al., 2013, op. cit.

80 Principals Australia Institute, *Australian principal certification program*, Principals Australia Institute, online, n.d, http://certification.pai.edu.au/, viewed 5 February 2015.

81 Copyright © 2014 Education Services Australia Limited as the legal entity for the COAG Education Council (Education Council). The Australian Council for Educational Research (ACER) has reproduced an extract of the Australian Professional Standard for Principals (2014) (Standard) in this publication with permission from the copyright owner. The Standard was developed by the Australian Institute for Teaching and School Leadership (AITSL) and endorsed by the Education Council. This publication is solely created by ACER and does not represent the views of, and is not endorsed by, AITSL or the Education Council, p.6

82 Australian Institute for Teaching and School Leadership, 2014, op. cit., p. 6.

83 See M Barber et al., 2010, op. cit.; C Day et al., op. cit.; S Dinham, 2005, op. cit.; S Dinham, *Leadership for exceptional educational outcomes*, Post Pressed, Teneriffe, Queensland, 2007b; S Dinham, 2008, op. cit.; S Dinham, 'Leadership for student achievement', in N Cranston & L Erlich (eds), *Australian educational school leadership today: issues and trends*, Australian Academic Press, Bowen Hills, Queensland, 2009; S Dinham, 2016, op. cit.; K Leithwood et al., 2010, op. cit.; D Reeves, 'Leadership and learning', *ACEL Monograph Series*, vol. 43, 2008, pp. 3–21; A Schleicher (ed), op. cit.; K L Wahlstrom et al., op. cit.

84 K Leithwood et al., 2002, pp. 863–75.

85 Hattie, J. (2009), p. 83.

86 S Dinham et al., 2013, op. cit.

87 S Dinham, *Pilot study to test the exposure draft of the national professional standard for principals: final report*, AITSL, Melbourne, 2011a.

88 This section is drawn from S Dinham, Chapter 19, 'What are the potential benefits of professional standards for school leaders?', 2016, pp. 305–17.

89 S Dinham et al., 2013, op. cit., p. 469; to note that 'Standards' was referred to in 2008, but later the singular 'Standard' was adopted as was the designation 'Principal'; the content in this extract has been informed by: S Dinham et al., 2008a, op. cit.; and S Dinham, L Ingvarson, E Kleinhenz, *Mapping of the common substance of graduate teacher standards developed and implemented by ATRA members against the MCEETYA framework for standards: development of graduate teacher standards Australia*, ACER Press, Melbourne, 2008b.

90 S Dinham et al., 2013, op. cit. p. 469; the content in this extract has been informed by S Dinham et al., 2009, op. cit., and S Dinham, 2008b, op. cit.

91 Australian Institute for Teaching and School Leadership, *National [Australian] professional standard for principals exposure draft*, AITSL, Melbourne, 2010.

92 M Barber et al., 2010, p. 3.

93 K Leithwood, C Day, P Sammons, A Harris & D Hopkins, *Seven strong claims about successful school leadership*, National College for School Leadership, Nottingham, 2006.

94 S Dinham, 2011, op. cit.

95 C Day et al., op. cit., p. 1.

96 Australian Institute for Teaching and School Leadership, 2014, op. cit., p. 11.

97 Australian Institute for Teaching and School Leadership, 2014, op. cit., p. 10.

98 S Dinham, 2011, op. cit.

99 Australian Institute for Teaching and School Leadership, 2014, op cit., pp. 10–11; to note that the three leadership requirements the standard is based on may be expressed as 'capabilities' in other standards and literature.

100 S Dinham, 2005, op. cit.

101 C Willig, *Introducing qualitative research methods in psychology*, McGraw Hill, Maidenhead, UK, 2008.

102 S Heath, R Brooks, E Cleaver & E Ireland, *Researching young people's lives*, Sage Publications, London, 2009.

103 J McLeod, 'Metaphors of the self: searching for young people's identity through interviews', in J McLeod & K Malone (eds), *Researching youth*, Australian Clearinghouse for Youth Studies, Hobart, 2000, pp. 45–8.

104 ibid.

105 S Chase, 'Narrative inquiry', in N Denzin & Y Lincoln (eds), *Handbook of qualitative research*, 3rd edn, Sage Publications, Thousand Oaks, 2005, pp. 651–79, p. 660.

106 N Denzin, *The research act: a theoretical introduction to sociological methods*, 3rd edn, Prentice Hall, Englewood Cliffs, NJ, 1989.

107 MB Miles & AM Huberman, *Qualitative data analysis*, 2nd edn, Sage Publications, Newbury Park, CA, 1994.

108 R K Yin, *Case study research: design and methods*, 4th edn, Sage Publications, Thousand Oaks, CA, 2009.

109 M B Miles et al., op. cit.

110 Australian Bureau of Statistics, *Schools Australia*, cat. no. 4221.0, ABS, Canberra, 2010, http://www.abs.gov.au/ausstats/abs@.nsf/Previousproducts/4221.0Main%20Features12010?opendocument&tabname=Summary&prodno=4221.0&issue=2010&num=&view=

111 Although there is a known phenomenon where men are less likely to attribute their success or abilities to others than is the case with women, so caution is advised with this comparison.

112 A number of principals preferred to speak of staff inclusively and included non-teachers; they were mindful of the important contribution of other administrative and support staff.

113 Ministerial Council on Education, Employment, Training and Youth Affairs, op. cit.

114 Australian Institute for Teaching and School Leadership, *National professional standards for teachers*, AITSL, Melbourne, 2011b; Australian Institute for Teaching and School Leadership, *Australian professional standards for teachers*, 2011c, https://www.aitsl.edu.au/teach/standards, viewed 12 February 2018.

115 Deloitte, *Principal workload and time use study*, report produced for the NSW Department of Education, September 2017, pp. 4–5. https://education.nsw.gov.au/media/schools-operation/Principal-workload-and-time-use-report.pdf

116 ibid., p. 5.

117 S Dinham, 2016, op. cit.

118 ibid.

119 V Robinson, *Reduce change to increase improvement*, Corwin, Thousand Oaks, CA, 2017.

120 When Dinham was leading the piloting of the Australian Professional Standard for Principals, one of the key pieces of feedback from principals was that the wellbeing aspects were underdone, and needed more attention and prominence. See S Dinham, 2011a, op. cit.

121 S Dinham, 2017, op. cit., Chapter 2.

APPENDIX
Interview Schedule Questions
[does not include demographic questions or prompts]

First Interview:
1. Tell me about why and what motivated you to become a principal?
2. Tell me about the culture you are developing for learning and teaching in your school?
3. Thinking about yourself personally and the task of leading teaching and learning in your school, where do you feel most capable and least adequate?
4. We are finishing this section on Leading teaching and learning, is there anything more you would like to say about leading teaching and learning in your school?
5. What do you think are important qualities of being a good school principal?
6. What were the main influences and contributors to developing your present capabilities and approaches to the principalship?
7. What knowledge and understanding do you believe assists you most in your role as principal?
8. How do you think others within and outside the school see you as a principal?
9. What is your view on professional learning and development of self and others?
10. What role should a principal play in the professional development of others? What strategies do you use to develop staff?

11. Thinking about yourself, given the role, how would you assess your current state of well-being? Do you have any particular strategies?
12. How would you assess the current state of personal well-being of staff at your school? What leadership strategies do you employ to address staff well-being?
13. We will bring the interview to a close now, is there anything more you would like to say about developing yourself and staff at your school?

Second Interview:

14. What is your vision for your school? What are you trying to achieve?
15. What are the three most important issues to be addressed at your school in the next five years?
16. What strategies do you employ to implement, monitor and measure the impact of school plans and policies?
17. Is there anything more you would like to add about leading improvement, innovation and change?
18. What data management methods do you use to ensure staff and resources are efficiently organised to provide an effective and safe learning environment?
19. Is there anything more you would like to say about leading the management of your school?
20. What are you working on with your school community? What strategies are you employing and how?
21. Is there anything more you would like to say about engaging and working with your school's community?
22. What would you like people to know about what it is like to be a principal?
23. What advice would you give a beginning principal? What do you wish you'd known when you started?
24. Is there anything more about being the principal or the principalship that you would like to add?

www.ingramcontent.com/pod-product-compliance
Lightning Source LLC
Chambersburg PA
CBHW052023070526
44584CB00016B/1882